Presented to:

_____

From:

_____

Date:

_____

Soul
Praise

Amazing Stories and Insights
Behind the Great African-American
Hymns and Negro Spirituals

HONOR ⊞ BOOKS

Inspiration and Motivation for the Seasons of Life

An Imprint of Cook Communications Ministries • Colorado Springs, CO

Unless otherwise noted, all Scripture quotations are taken from the *King James Version* of the Bible.

09 08 07 06 05   10 9 8 7 6 5 4 3 2 1

Soul Praise—
Amazing Stories and Insights Behind the Great
African-American Hymns and Negro Spirituals
ISBN 1-56292-343-9

Copyright © 2005 Bordon Books
6532 E. 71st Street, Suite 105
Tulsa, OK 74133

Published by Honor Books,
An Imprint of Cook Communications Ministries
4050 Lee Vance View
Colorado Springs, CO 80918

Developed by Bordon Books

Manuscript written by Ronald C. Jordan
Cover designed by Koechel Peterson and Associates

SOUL
PRAISE

AMAZING STORIES AND INSIGHTS
BEHIND THE GREAT AFRICAN-AMERICAN
HYMNS AND NEGRO SPIRITUALS

INTRODUCTION

Soul Praise—Amazing Stories and Insights Behind the Great African-American Hymns and Negro Spirituals explores the people, places, and events that have shaped the heart and soul of African-American worship music. The powerful, soul-stirring songs are familiar—*Swing, Low Sweet Chariot; Go Down, Moses; Take My Hand, Precious Lord.* These anthems are rooted in the richness of African-American history and continue to offer solace and celebration to hearts seeking freedom and hope.

Soul Praise is divided into the following sections:

Traditional Spirituals covers the period before 1865 when Negro spirituals, or plantations songs as they were also called, had their beginnings in the deep recesses of southern fields. Instructions for secret meetings and planned escapes were often hidden in the lyrics of these songs. Slaves used them to communicate even under the watchful eye of their unsuspecting masters.

Beyond Abolition: Black Renaissance/Civil Rights Movement covers the period between 1865 and 1960 and takes a look at some of the works of such noted composers as Thomas A. Dorsey, Charles A. Tindley, and Lucie Campbell. Also included in this section is a sampling of songs made popular during the Civil Rights Movement of the 1960s.

Euro-American Contributors, the third section, gives more insight into the works of Watts, brothers Charles and John Wesley, John Newton, and other Euro-Americans who penned many of the hymns sung in African-American churches. Just as African Americans took the Christian religion as their own, they also embraced some of its music—breathing new life into it and adapting it to their history, culture, and circumstances.

Soul Praise will captivate and inspire you to reach out with personal faith and praise to the God of your fathers. It will also encourage you to deepen the roots of your faith and help you celebrate the fortitude, hope, and faith behind songs that continue to enrich the world of music.

Part I

Slave &
Plantation Songs:

Traditional Spirituals Before 1865

The history of the Negro spirituals, also referred to as slave songs and plantation songs, is more than a simple accounting of the foundation of African-American music in this country. It is a story with much deeper roots—roots that reach back in time to reveal the sordid tale of a torturous human bondage—a time when African Americans were held captive and struggled to survive the tyranny of their white slave owners. Many slaves lost that struggle along the way, but their struggle lives on through the testimony of song.

The old Negro spirituals give an account of the life and history of Black Americans and how they suffered enslavement and persecution solely because of their skin color. Sometimes the songs were joyous, but many times they were sad. The lyrics almost always served as testimonies of a people who had strong faith that their God would someday deliver them.

"They are the music of an unhappy people, of the children of disappointment," the 19th-century writer and educator W.E.B. DuBois wrote in his book, *The Souls of Black Folks*. "They tell of death and suffering, and unvoiced longing toward a truer world, of misty wanderings and hidden ways."

Examples can be found in songs such as *Steal Away*, a traditional plantation spiritual that speaks of the desire of every African American entrapped by the bonds of slavery. "Steal away, steal away, steal away to Jesus! Steal away, steal away home, I ain't got long to stay here." The hope was always for a way of escape from their present hardships, a "stealing away" to refuge in the arms of a loving Savior. Until that final refuge could be found, the slaves found solace in allowing their spirits to steal away during their secret religious meetings.

Often, the slaves looked to the Bible and the stories of the Israelites' escape from bondage for inspiration and encouragement. Much of that inspiration is reflected in the lyrics of songs like *Go Down, Moses; Michael, Row the Boat Ashore;* and *Joshua Fit the Battle of Jerico.* These songs illustrate a strong hope for freedom and deliverance and an eventual resting place in their own Promised Land.

GO DOWN, MOSES

H.T. BURLEIGH

Go down, Moses
Way down in Egypt land,
Tell ole Pharaoh,
To let my people go.

When Israel was in Egypt's land,
Let my people go,
Oppressed so hard they could not stand,
Let my people go.

"Thus spoke the Lord," bold Moses said;
Let my people go.
"If not, I'll smite your first born dead,"
Let my people go.

No more shall they in bondage toil,
Let my people go,
Let them come out with Egypt's spoil,
Let my people go.

When Israel out of Egypt came,
Let my people go,
And left the proud oppressive land,
Let my people go.

O, 'twas a dark and dismal night,
Let my people go,
When Moses led the Israelites,
Let my people go.

'Twas good ole Moses and Aaron, too,

Let my people go,
'Twas they that led the armies through,
Let my people go.

The Lord told Moses what to do,
Let my people go,
To lead the children of Israel through,
Let my people go.

O come along, Moses, you'll not get lost,
Let my people go,
Stretch out your rod and come across,
Let my people go.

As Israel stood by the waterside,
Let my people go,
At the command of God it did divide,
Let my people go.

When they had reached the other shore,
Let my people go,
They sang a song of triumph o'er,
Let my people go.

Go down, Moses
Way down in Egypt land,
Tell ole Pharaoh,
To let my people go.

During the dark days of slavery, planned escapes and secret gatherings could not be discussed in the open. Instead, slaves often concealed secret messages or double meanings in the songs that they sang while working. Oftentimes the slaves sang these songs in the very presence of unsuspecting masters.

The spiritual *Go Down, Moses* is a classic example of one that carried a double meaning. On the surface, the song relates the powerful story of Moses from the book of Exodus as he leads the Israelites out of Egypt after delivering God's profound message to Pharaoh: "Let My people go." As God's chosen people, the Israelites had undergone severe testing at the hands of Pharaoh and the Egyptians. Therefore, this song proclaimed a message of permanent deliverance from the chains of bondage and freedom to cross over into the slaves' own "Promised Land."

In addition, the Biblical characters portrayed in some of these spirituals may have been representative of contemporary figures. Moses, for example, may have referred to Christ—the One who came to deliver His people from their sin. But more likely, the figure of Moses represented Harriet Tubman, who led hundreds of slaves to freedom through the Underground Railroad. Pharaoh, of course, could have been analogous to the slaves' evil masters, who refused to hear the voice of God and release the captives.

As this powerful song describes the Hebrews' release from bondage, it likens their freedom to the redemption of humanity through the suffering and victory of Christ on the Cross. Through their singing, the slaves expressed their hope that God would someday send a "Moses" into their "Egypt" and secure their escape from bondage and lead them into the Promised Land.

THERE IS A BALM IN GILEAD

There is a balm in Gilead
To make the wounded whole;
There is a balm in Gilead
To heal the sin-sick soul.

Sometimes I feel discouraged,
And think my work's in vain,
But then the Holy Spirit
Revives my soul again.

There is a balm in Gilead
To make the wounded whole;
There is a balm in Gilead
To heal the sin-sick soul.

If you can't preach like Peter,
If you can't pray like Paul,
Just tell the love of Jesus,
And say He died for all.

There is a balm in Gilead
To make the wounded whole;
There is a balm in Gilead
To heal the sin-sick soul.

These comforting lyrics, written by an author who remains unknown to this day, answer the longing question asked by the prophet Jeremiah: "Is there no balm in Gilead; is there no physician there? Why then is not the health of the daughter of my people recovered?" (Jeremiah 8:22).

Jeremiah posed this question while grieving over the people of Israel, who had turned their backs on God and refused to repent. Those African Americans who sang this song responded that, yes, "There is a balm in Gilead to make the wounded whole. There is a balm in Gilead to heal the sin-sick soul."

That balm, of course, is Jesus—the One who paid the price for all that they had suffered and continue to suffer. The faith of those African Americans in bondage rested in their belief that the God who saves is also the God who heals and delivers. It was their belief that no matter how strong the oppression or how heavy the burden, God would eventually free them. They found comfort in knowing He would bring healing—to both spirit and soul. This song also bears a timeless message for us today. Christ's death at Calvary is our assurance that deliverance has already come. Not only did Jesus die for your sins, but His resurrection provides freedom from those sins.

OH, FREEDOM

Oh, freedom
Oh, freedom
Oh, freedom over me!
And before I'd be a slave
I'll be buried in my grave
And go home to my Lord and be free.
No more moaning
No more moaning
No more moaning over me!
And before I'd be a slave
I'll be buried in my grave
And go home to my Lord and be free.

There'll be singing
There'll be singing
There'll be singing over me!
And before I'd be a slave
I'll be buried in my grave
And go home to my Lord and be free.

There'll be shouting
There'll be shouting
There'll be shouting over me!
And before I'd be a slave
I'll be buried in my grave
And go home to my Lord and be free.

There'll be praying
There'll be praying
There'll be praying over me!
And before I'd be a slave
I'll be buried in my grave
And go home to my Lord and be free.

Booker T. Washington, in examining the roots of African and African-American music, said: "There is a difference between the music of Africa and that of her transplanted children. There is a new note in the music which had its origin in the southern plantation, and in this new note the sorrow and sufferings which came from serving in a strange land found expression."[1]

Adding to that, Garner C. Taylor went on to say, "A part, perhaps the major part, of that 'new note' came from the Black sufferers' particular and circumstantial viewing of the Christian faith, which was so different from what the slave masters and their religious agents had intended in the way they had presented the biblical revelation to the slave community, . . . The owners spoke of slavery being 'God-ordained'; the slaves heard, 'Before I'd be a slave, I'd be buried in my grave.'"[2]

This powerful declaration sung decades ago spoke clearly the sentiment of those trapped in the bonds of slavery whose hearts cried out to experience freedom—a freedom that would be realized only in death. Such freedom, they felt, would result in rejoicing by those left behind. They would not moan, but would be found singing, shouting, and praying over the one who had been delivered.

Considered one of many "message songs" sung by slaves, *Oh, Freedom* served to help African Americans hold on to their humanity, giving them hope even of an earthly freedom. The song was also popular during the Civil

Rights Movement and was sung by many who waged constant battle against more sophisticated forms of slavery, such as job discrimination and racial profiling.

During an interview in which he discussed the making of the black civil rights film *Freedom Song* (2000), Chuck McDew, a former chairman of the Student Nonviolent Coordinating Committee (SNCC), explained the reasoning behind the movie's title:

"The first Freedom Song dates back to slavery," he said. "When the first slaves who were brought to the islands off the coast of Georgia were getting off the boat, they began to sing a song, which translated to:

> *'Oh Freedom, Oh Freedom over me, over me.*
> *And before I'd be a slave, I'd be buried in my grave*
> *And go home to my Lord and be free.'*

"Then, they just turned around and walked right back into the water and drowned themselves. They said 'the water took us here and the water is going to take us away.' They would rather be dead than slaves."[3]

According to McDew, slaves on the mainland heard the words to the song and began to sing it in English. Like the film, *Oh, Freedom* demonstrates that the struggle for freedom—the freedom to be treated equal in every respect—is ongoing.

JOSHUA FIT THE BATTLE OF JERICO

Joshua fit the battle of Jerico, Jerico, Jerico,
Joshua fit the battle of Jerico,
And the walls came tumbling down.

Joshua fit the battle of Jerico, Jerico, Jerico,
Joshua fit the battle of Jerico,
an' de walls came tumbling down.

You may talk about de King of Gideon,
You may talk about de King of Saul,
There's none like good ol' Joshua,
At de battle of Jerico.

Joshua fit the battle of Jerico, Jerico, Jerico,
Joshua fit the battle of Jerico,
And the walls came tumbling down.

Right up to the walls of Jerico,
He marched with spear in hand.
"Go blow them ram horns," Joshua cried,
"Cause the battle is in my hand."

Joshua fit the battle of Jerico, Jerico, Jerico,
Joshua fit the battle of Jerico,
And the walls came tumbling down.

Then Joshua had the people blow,
And the trumpets with mighty sound,
And they blew so awful loud and long,
That the walls came tumblin' down.
That the walls came tumblin' down,
Tumblin' down.

Joshua fit the battle of Jerico, Jerico, Jerico,
Joshua fit the battle of Jerico,
And the walls came tumbling down.

Joshua Fit the Battle of Jerico reads as a proclamation that as long as the slaves retained their faith and trusted God to deliver them, they were not far from reaching their precious "Promised Land." The tumbling of the walls may have signified the eventual crumbling of the walls of slavery that enclosed them and the opening of a passageway by which they could march to freedom.

As previously mentioned, slaves often looked to the story of the Israelites' escape from bondage as a metaphor for their own eventual deliverance. For them, the Promised Land represented freedom from slavery. It was their hope to one day see their own deliverance.

STEAL AWAY TO JESUS

Steal away, steal away, steal away to Jesus!
Steal away, steal away home,
I ain't got long to stay here.

My Lord, He calls me,
He calls me by the thunder;
The trumpet sounds within my soul,
I ain't got long to stay here.

Steal away, steal away, steal away to Jesus!
Steal away, steal away home,
I ain't got long to stay here.

Green trees are bending,
Poor sinners stand a-trembling;
The trumpet sounds within my soul,
I ain't got long to stay here.

Steal away, steal away, steal away to Jesus!
Steal away, steal away home,
I ain't got long to stay here.

My Lord, He calls me,
He calls me by the lightning;
The trumpet sounds within my soul,
I ain't got long to stay here.

This traditional African-American spiritual, often referred to as a southern plantation melody, tells of the desire of every Black entrapped in the bonds of slavery.

They were certain that their time on earth was short. The hope was to escape, to "steal away" to refuge in the arms of a loving Savior. This refuge might have taken place in death. But in life, the slaves stole away to their secret religious meetings and found refuge.

One of the many "signal" or message songs sung by the slaves, the lyrics of this song were not always sung. Sometimes a slave group leader might hum the first few words to someone else in the group, who would in turn hum them to someone else. This pattern would sometimes go on all day, even within earshot of the unsuspecting master, until everyone had been made aware of a pending meeting. Slave revolt leader Nat Turner is said to have used this song to call his co-conspirators together.

Frederick Douglass once explained that an attentive observer would have been able to see in the repetition of such lyrics as "O Canaan, sweet Canaan, I'm goin' to the land of Canaan" something more than the hope to reach Heaven. In those lyrics the singer expressed the hope of reaching the North, which was seen as Canaan.

Today, as it was then, many who have grown tired of life and all its troubles sing of a time when they can "steal away"—a time when they can "go home and be with the Lord." For them, the promise of escape is to a glorious place called Heaven.

SWING LOW, SWEET CHARIOT

H.T. BURLEIGH

I looked over Jordan and what did I see
coming for to carry me home?
A band of angels coming after me,
Coming for to carry me home.

Swing low, sweet chariot, coming for to carry
me home. Swing low, sweet chariot, coming for
to carry me home.

If you get there before I do,
Coming for to carry me home.
Tell all my friends I'm a coming too,
Coming for to carry me home.

I'm sometimes up and sometimes down
coming for to carry me home.
But still my soul is heavenly bound
coming for to carry me home.

Religion's like a blooming rose,
Coming for to carry me home.
None can't tell it but dem dat knows,
Coming for to carry me home.

Although frequently used as lullaby lyrics, this song is best recognized for its direct relationship to the Underground Railroad and its symbolism for slaves seeking escape. Slaves sought flight from persecution by several means. The Underground Railroad, an elaborate system linking a vast network of people who helped fugitive slaves escape to the North and to Canada, was a major method. Through the use of this network, made up of many individuals—including many whites—who knew only of the local efforts to aid fugitives and not of the overall operation, thousands of slaves escaped to freedom.

Throughout the lyrics of slave songs, there are references to many different modes of travel—realistic and otherwise. Included are chariots, trains, water, ships, and even wings as indicated in one song titled *Now Let Me Fly*. The image of the "sweet chariot" in *Swing Low, Sweet Chariot* comes directly from the story in Second Kings of the prophet Elijah being caught up by God and swept away in a chariot to heaven. "As they [Elijah and Elisha] continued walking and talking, a chariot of fire and horses of fire separated the two of them, and Elijah ascended in a whirlwind into heaven" (2 Kings 2:11 NRSV).

Obviously, there existed no such chariot. However, a sled-like device known as a chariot was reportedly once used by enslaved workers in the Carolinas to transport tobacco. It is likely that "chariot" was coded language for "train," which at the time was the most modern means of transportation. Then, as now, neither chariots nor trains are sufficient to assure passage into Heaven. Yet the song serves as inspiration that a place has been prepared for the believer and Jesus will show him how to get there.

GO TELL IT ON THE MOUNTAIN

Go tell it on the mountain,
O'er the hills and everywhere.
Go tell it on the mountain,
That Jesus Christ is born.

When I was a sinner,
I prayed both day and night.
I asked the Lord to help me
And He showed me the way.
(chorus)

When I was a seeker,
I sought both night and day.
I asked the Lord to help me
and He taught me to pray.
(chorus)

He made me a watchman
Up on the city wall.
And if I am a Christian,
I am the least of all.
(chorus)

Christmas held a very prominent place in the hearts of the slaves for a number of reasons. First, it celebrated the birth of Jesus Christ. Second, it was considered a "carnival season" for these children of bondage who knew no freedom or time of celebration. It was the only time during the entire year when they were allowed a little restricted liberty.

While the author of this spiritual is unknown, former slave Solomon Northup gives us a glimpse of the jubilation the slaves experienced during this special time of the year. "The only respite from constant labor the slave has through the whole year is during the Christmas holidays. Epps (a planter) allowed us three—others allow four, five, and six days, according to the measure of their generosity. It is the only time to which they look forward with any interest or pleasure. They are glad when night comes, not only because it brings them a few hours repose, but because it brings them one day nearer Christmas . . . the time of feasting, and frolicking, and fiddling—the carnival season with the children of bondage. They are the only days when they are allowed a little restricted liberty, and heartily indeed do they enjoy it."[4]

One of only a handful of spiritual hymns tied specifi-cally to Christmas, this one was a favorite. A joyful tune filled with hope and expectation, this song has become a contemporary Christmas favorite as well.

WALK IN JERUSALEM (I WANT TO BE READY)

I want to be ready, I want to be ready,
I want to be ready, to walk in Jerusalem just like John.
John said the city was just foursquare,
Walk in Jerusalem just like John.
And he declared he'd meet me there,
Walk in Jerusalem just like John.

I want to be ready, I want to be ready,
I want to be ready, to walk in Jerusalem just like John.
O John, O John, what do you say?
Walk in Jerusalem just like John.
That I'll be there at the coming day,
Walk in Jerusalem just like John.

I want to be ready, I want to be ready,
I want to be ready, to walk in Jerusalem just like John.
When Peter was preaching at Pentecost,
Walk in Jerusalem just like John.
He was endowed with the Holy Ghost,
Walk in Jerusalem just like John.

I want to be ready, I want to be ready,
I want to be ready, to walk in Jerusalem just like John.
If you get there before I do,
Walk in Jerusalem just like John.
Tell all my friends I'm a-comin', too,
Walk in Jerusalem just like John.

I want to be ready, I want to be ready,
I want to be ready, to walk in Jerusalem just like John.

While seeking freedom on earth, it was the hope of every African-American slave to someday reach that heavenly home, to someday walk on the streets of gold, to see that Holy City that John describes as, "the holy city, new Jerusalem, coming down from God out of heaven, prepared as a bride adorned for her husband" (Revelation 21:2).

Believing that their Lord could come at any time, these believers wanted to make sure they were always prepared—ready to go when the Lord came to take them away to Heaven. There they would be reunited with loved ones who had gone on before them. They would walk the streets of gold and dwell in the presence of such men as John the Baptist. These enslaved men and women knew that, as the apostle Paul said, to go to Heaven was to go and be with the Lord Jesus. After a life of struggle and distress, their desire was to someday join that heavenly band of angels and stand in the presence of their Lord. That meant they had to stay ready like the five virgins who always kept oil in the lamps in anticipation of the bridegroom's arrival. (See Matthew 25.)

We have this same hope that when our course is finished, when the race is run, we will see Jesus and hear Him say, "Well done." Jesus' time of return is not known, but it is promised. And when He returns, He will be looking for a church that is ready—in every way.

WERE YOU THERE?

Were you there when they crucified my Lord?
Were you there when they crucified my Lord?
O sometimes it causes me to tremble, tremble, tremble,
Were you there when they crucified my Lord?

Were you there when they nailed Him to the tree?
Were you there when they nailed Him to the tree?
O sometimes it causes me to tremble, tremble, tremble,
Were you there when they crucified my Lord?

Were you there when they pierced Him in the side?
Were you there when they pierced Him in the side?
O sometimes it causes me to tremble, tremble, tremble,
Were you there when they crucified my Lord?

Were you there when the sun refused to shine?
Were you there when the sun refused to shine?
O sometimes it causes me to tremble, tremble, tremble,
Were you there when they crucified my Lord?

Were you there when they laid Him in the tomb?
Were you there when they laid Him in the tomb?
O sometimes it causes me to tremble, tremble, tremble,
Were you there when they crucified my Lord?

The question in this popular spiritual begs a
response—one that no one can escape. Were you there? In
the natural, the answer would be "no." But spiritually, we
all were there—represented by our sin and shame taken on
by the Son of God who died so that we all may live. No

doubt this was on the mind of the unknown author who penned this beautifully-written hymn, whose words so reach the depths of our soul and reveal the shame and guilt that we all have.

The song symbolizes the story of the Crucifixion of Jesus Christ—the brutal torture that preceded His death, burial, and resurrection—and leads us through each painful moment. We hear the striking of the nails as they are driven into His hands and feet, and we feel the stabbing pain that follows the piercing in His side by a Roman soldier's sword.

This dramatic song puts us right in the middle—to witness the sacrifice Jesus Christ made for the sake of all man. And yes, it causes us to tremble! What love one must have to endure such pain and agony. This song also serves as a reminder that the Savior, who gave His life for all, still lives. Fear and trembling were overcome by victory and praise as the stone was rolled away and Jesus Christ rose from the dead.

THIS TRAIN IS BOUND FOR GLORY

This train is bound for glory, this train,
This train is bound for glory, this train,
This train is bound for glory,
Don't ride nothin' but the righteous an' the glory,
This train is bound for glory, this train.

This train don't carry gamblers, this train,
This train don't carry gamblers, this train,
This train don't carry gamblers,
No hypocrites, no midnight ramblers,
This train is bound for glory, this train.

This train is build for speed now, this train,
This train is build for speed now, this train,
This train is build for speed,
Fastest train you ever did see,
This train is bound for glory, this train.

This train don't carry no liars, this train,
This train don't carry no liars, this train,
This train don't carry no liars,
No hypocrites and no high flyers,
This train is bound for glory, this train.

This train don't pay no transportation, this train,
This train don't pay no transportation, this train,
This train don't pay no transportation,
No Jim Crow and no discrimination,
This train is bound for glory, this train.

This train don't carry no rustlers, this train,
This train don't carry no rustlers, this train,
This train don't carry no rustlers,
Sidestreet walkers, two-bit hustlers,
This train is bound for glory, this train.

As with a number of older spirituals, this one has several versions that suggest different meanings. Another version, for instance, includes the words "This train is bound for glory, get on board, and tell your story."

As the "conductor" led the slaves on the Underground Railroad, it was understood that everyone who was "on board" had to tell their story. In the context of a praise meeting, "telling your story" meant testifying about the trials and tribulations of life and thanking the Almighty for giving the guidance to overcome obstacles and burdens.

These testimonials served as an inspiration for others to follow in your footsteps and trust in God. A subsequent meaning of "tell your story" meant that once you reached freedom, you were obligated to tell the story of your life in slavery, your escape, and your ultimate freedom, so that the events could be documented to further the anti-slavery cause.

Today, many churches still incorporate testimonies like these into their services to give people the opportunity to share what God has done for them. Such services inspire others who may be facing similar hardships.

NOBODY KNOWS THE TROUBLE I'VE SEEN

ARRANGED BY H.T. BURLEIGH

Nobody knows the trouble I've seen,
Nobody knows but Jesus.
Nobody knows the trouble I've seen,
Glory, Hallelujah!

Sometimes I'm up, sometimes I'm down,
Oh, yes, Lord!
Sometimes I'm almost to the ground,
Oh, yes, Lord!

Nobody knows the trouble I've seen,
Nobody knows but Jesus.
Nobody knows the trouble I've seen,
Glory, Hallelujah!

I never shall forget that day,
Oh, yes, Lord!
When Jesus washed my sins away,
Oh, yes, Lord!

Nobody knows the trouble I've seen,
Nobody knows but Jesus.
Nobody knows the trouble I've seen,
Glory, Hallelujah!

Although you see me goin' so
Oh, yes, Lord!
I have my trials here below,
Oh, yes, Lord!

Nobody knows the trouble I've seen,
Nobody knows but Jesus.
Nobody knows the trouble I've seen,
Glory, Hallelujah!

The musical influence that led the accomplished musician and composer Harry Thacker Burleigh to write such moving hymns as *Nobody Knows the Trouble I've Seen* can be traced as far back as his grandfather. Often, young Burleigh would listen as Hamilton Waters, a partially blind ex-slave who had run away and settled in Pennsylvania, sing some of the old Negro spirituals and plantation songs.

But Burleigh also drew from the experiences of his mother, an educated woman who was fluent in both French and Greek but who had become a domestic worker because she was unable to get a job teaching. Even his own struggles while growing up played a part in the songs Burleigh would later write.

"I used to stand hungry in front of one of Dennett's downtown restaurants and watch the man in the window cook cakes," Burleigh recalled of a time around 1892 when he was a music student and his scholarship covered only tuition. "Then I would take a toothpick from my pocket, use it as if I had eaten, draw on my imagination, and walk down the street singing to myself."

Years later, Burleigh graduated from the National Conservatory of Music in New York and went on to write more than 300 of the most popular, heartfelt songs and hymns the church has ever heard, including *Deep River, Go Down, Moses,* and *Swing Low, Sweet Chariot.*

Nobody Knows the Trouble I've Seen is a testament to the lives and struggles of the slaves Burleigh heard about in the songs his grandfather sang. A timeless spiritual that continues to touch lives as strongly today as when Burleigh wrote it during the early 1900s, the work possesses many of the same themes as other spirituals—describing the intense feelings of sorrow, hurt, loneliness, and oppression experienced in life. It also offers comfort and hope through the assurance that Jesus knows and understands. It is a reminder to do as Jesus recommends: "Come to Me . . . and I will give you rest" (Matthew 11:28 NLT).

I'm a Soldier in the Army of the Lord

I'm a soldier in the army of the Lord
I'm a soldier in the army
I'm a soldier in the army of the Lord
I'm a soldier in the army
I'm a soldier in the army of the Lord
I'm a soldier in the army
I'm a soldier in the army of the Lord
I'm a soldier in the army

I got my war clothes on in the army of the Lord
I got my war clothes on in the army
I got my war clothes on in the army of the Lord
I got my war clothes on in the army
(chorus)

I believe I'll die in the army of the Lord
I believe I'll die in the army
I believe I'll die in the army of the Lord
I believe I'll die in the army
(chorus)

I got my breastplate on in the army of the Lord
Got my breastplate on in the army
I got my breastplate on in the army of the Lord
I got my breastplate on in the army
(chorus)

I'm gonna fight until I die in the army of the Lord
I'm gonna fight until I die in the army of the Lord
I'm gonna fight until I die in the army of the Lord
Gonna fight until I die in the army of the Lord
(chorus)

Ain't gonna be no turning back in the army of the Lord
Ain't gonna be no turning back in the army
Ain't gonna be no turning back in the army of the Lord
Gonna be no turning back in the army of the Lord
(chorus)

Although dreams of the "sweet by and by" helped slaves cope with their sufferings, reality in their day-to-day existence was continual bondage. Focused on the hope that one day they would find deliverance, it became an obvious duty for them to take a stand on their faith in God and recognize that they were in a battle for their lives.

Such thoughts gave rise to songs that suggested that while they were on the earth, their position was to stand firm in their faith. Often, the lyrics proclaimed their intentions or described how they lived their lives. Words such as watch, fight, and pray in this song were very significant to the stance the slaves took while in bondage.

If there was an escape planned, the slaves had to be observant and vigilant regarding the habits of their masters. Daytime was the domain of the owner, so nighttime became the haven for the slaves. Lyrics such as "I got my war clothes on," "I believe I'll die," and "Ain't gonna be no turning back in the army of the Lord" in the song, *I'm a Soldier in the Army of the Lord,* suggest a strong determination on their part not to give up, but to hold out and fight to the finish.

EVERY TIME I FEEL THE SPIRIT

Every time I feel the spirit . . .
Moving in my heart I will pray.
Every time I feel the spirit
Moving in my heart I will pray.

Upon a mountain my Lord spoke,
Out of his mouth came fire and smoke.
Down in the valley on my knees,
I asked the Lord have mercy please.

Every time I feel the spirit . . .
Moving in my heart I will pray.
Every time I feel the spirit
Moving in my heart I will pray.

Jordan river chilly and cold,
Took my body but not my soul.
All around me looking so fine,
I ask the Lord and know it is mine.

Every time I feel the spirit . . .
Moving in my heart I will pray.
Every time I feel the spirit
Moving in my heart I will pray.

Ain't but one train runs this track,
Runs to heaven runs right back.
St. Peter waiting at the gate,
Saying come on sinner, don't be late.

Every time I feel the spirit . . .
Moving in my heart I will pray.

Every time I feel the spirit,
Moving in my heart I will pray.

Sinner, don't be late.
Sinner, don't be late.
Sinner, don't be late.
Sinner, don't be late.

Every time I feel the spirit . . .
Moving in my heart I will pray.
Every time I feel the spirit,
Moving in my heart I will pray.

Often, the songs sung by the slaves reflected personal needs or experiences. Feelings and emotions had a lot to do with how close they felt to God and how He made His presence known to them. It was not hard for them to sense His presence.

In recalling his experiences while living on a plantation in Texas, 100-year-old former slave Richard Carruthers remembered a time when the slaves would "have a prayin' ground down in the hollow."

"Sometime we come out of the field, between 11 and 12 at night, scorchin' and burnin' up with nothin' to eat, and we wants to ask the good Lawd to have mercy," Carruthers remembered. "We puts grease in a snuff pan or bottle and make a lamp. We takes a pine torch, too, and goes down in the hollow to pray. Some gits so joyous they starts to holler loud and we has to stop up they mouth. I see [some people]

git so full of the Lawd and so happy they draps uncon-
scious."[5]

In similar fashion, praise and worship music exudes a
similar response in many African-American churches
today, because people can enter into the presence of God.
Prayer is also constant and continuous as worshipers seek
a closer relationship with God.

Every Time I Feel the Spirit, with lyrics that include
"Down in the valley on my knees, I asked the Lord have
mercy please," speaks of such a personal and direct relationship with God—a sensing of His presence that is ushered in by prayer and meditation or the singing of spiritual
songs.

IT'S ME, O LORD (STANDING IN THE NEED OF PRAYER)

It's me, it's me, it's me, O Lord
Standing in the need of prayer.
It's me, it's me, it's me, O Lord
Standing in the need of prayer.

Not my brother, not my sister, but it's me O Lord
Standing in the need of prayer.
Not my brother, not my sister, but it's me O Lord
Standing in the need of prayer.

It's me, it's me, it's me, O Lord
Standing in the need of prayer.
It's me, it's me, it's me, O Lord
Standing in the need of prayer.

Not the preacher, not the sinner, but it's me O Lord
Standing in the need of prayer.
Not the preacher, not the sinner, but it's me O Lord
Standing in the need of prayer.

It's me, it's me, it's me, O Lord
Standing in the need of prayer.
It's me, it's me, it's me, O Lord
Standing in the need of prayer.

Not my mother, not my father, but it's me O Lord
Standing in the need of prayer.
Not my mother, not my father, but it's me O Lord
Standing in the need of prayer.

It's me, it's me, it's me, O Lord
Standing in the need of prayer.
It's me, it's me, it's me, O Lord
Standing in the need of prayer.

The idea behind this song is simple—pray for me. The request comes not for someone else— not brother or sister, not preacher or sinner, not father or mother—but as the petitioner declares before God, "It's me, O Lord, standing in the need of prayer."

Another song taken straight from the scriptures, this petition directly relates to the command of God that His people pray for one another. The promise here is that prayer offered in faith will heal the sick and the Lord will make them well. In addition, anyone who has committed sins will be forgiven (James 5:16 NLT).

To the slaves, prayer was always important. It was wonderful when they could come together, in secret or in times approved by their masters, and talk to the God who watched over them—the One who would eventually bring them deliverance. Their prayers could not be hindered by the masters and would always be heard by God. It brought peace to troubled souls and comfort in what often seemed like hopeless situations.

The same is true today, not only for those who suffer oppression but also for those seeking a relationship with God. The command that we pray is still the same. Just as He heard the prayers of those in bondage, God hears our prayers today.

WE ARE CLIMBING JACOB'S LADDER

We are climbing Jacob's ladder,
We are climbing Jacob's ladder,
We are climbing Jacob's ladder,
Soldiers of the cross.

Every round goes higher, higher,
Every round goes higher, higher,
Every round goes higher, higher,
Soldiers of the cross.

Sinner, do you love my Jesus?
Sinner, do you love my Jesus?
Sinner, do you love my Jesus?
Soldiers of the cross.

If you love Him, why not serve Him?
If you love Him, why not serve Him?
If you love Him, why not serve Him?
Soldiers of the cross.

This is another well-known hymn taken directly from an Old Testament story of struggle which speaks as much to the individual as it does to a collective group. The dream Jacob had about the ladder is recorded in the book of Genesis:

"As he slept, he dreamed of a stairway that reached from earth to heaven. And he saw the angels of God going up and down on it. At the top of the stairway stood the

Lord, and he said, 'I am the Lord, the God of your grandfather Abraham and the God of your father, Isaac. The ground you are lying on belongs to you. I will give it to you and your descendants. What's more, I will be with you, and I will protect you wherever you go. I will someday bring you safely back to this land. I will be with you constantly until I have finished giving you everything I have promised.' Then Jacob woke up and said, 'Surely the Lord is in this place, and I wasn't even aware of it . . . It is none other than the house of God—the gateway to heaven.'" (Genesis 28:12-13, 15-17 NLT).

There are several interpretations of what this dream signifies. Why, for instance, were the angels going up and down the ladder? And why was God standing above the ladder? Jacob recognized the ladder as the "gate of Heaven." Perhaps the slaves did as well. But without sufficient teaching, the uneducated slaves were left to their own interpretation of the Bible. They knew enough to recognize the many promises given throughout God's Word and there were certainly some recorded in this story.

God identified himself as their Lord and promised that they and their children would be blessed. He also promised to be with them and to keep them wherever they went. What a word of comfort to those in trouble, bondage, distress, or despair. God's blessings are endless, and His promise is always the same: "I am with you always, even until the end of the world" (Matthew 28:20).

I Got Wings (All God's Chillun Got Wings)

I got wings, you got wings,
All o' God's children got wings.
When I get to Heaven, gonna put on my wings
And gonna fly all over God's Heaven, Heaven, Heaven.
Every talkin' 'bout Heaven ain't goin' there;
Heaven, gonna fly all over God's Heaven.

I got shoes, you got shoes,
All o' God's children got shoes.
When I get to Heaven, gonna put on my shoes
And gonna walk all over God's Heaven, Heaven, Heaven.
Every talkin' 'bout Heaven ain't goin' there;
Heaven, gonna walk all over God's Heaven.

I got a harp, you got a harp,
All o' God's children got a harp.
When I get to Heaven, gonna put on my harp
And gonna play all over God's Heaven, Heaven, Heaven.
Every talkin' 'bout Heaven ain't goin' there;
Heaven, gonna play all over God's Heaven.

I got a robe, you got a robe,
All o' God's children got a robe.
When I get to Heaven, gonna put on my robe
And gonna shout all over God's Heaven, Heaven, Heaven.
Every talkin' 'bout Heaven ain't goin' there;
Heaven, gonna shout all over God's Heaven.

Just as the Bible gave slaves a picture of what Heaven would be like, they also gained an interpretation of what they, as "Heavenly citizens," would look like. They may have been little valued on earth, but their citizenry in Heaven would afford them a new, regal look, including new clothing. They took joy in knowing that whatever they lacked on earth would be supplied by their Heavenly Father when they reached their Heavenly home. They delighted in singing about it:

> *I got shoes, you got shoes,*
> *All o' God's children got shoes.*
> *When I get to Heaven, gonna put on my shoes*
> *And gonna walk all over God's Heaven.*

There would even be a robe—a sign of royalty—to wear and a harp that could be used to play songs of worship and praise to God. And they believed they would have wings. No more walking barefooted, suffering blisters and sores. Now they could "fly all over God's Heaven."

While it is not known for certain, the line repeated in each verse that says, "Every talkin' 'bout Heaven ain't goin' there," may have been an indirect indictment against the many slave masters who, though they were churchgoers, did not live lives that were consistent with that action.

A song filled with faith and expectancy, its words still ring true today for those who trust in God, the Author of our faith.

DEEP RIVER

H.T. BURLEIGH

Deep river, my home is over Jordan,
Deep river, Lord, I want to cross over into campground.
Deep river, my home is over Jordan,
Deep river, Lord, I want to cross over into campground.
Oh, don't you want to go to that gospel feast,
That promised land where all is peace?
Oh deep river, Lord, I want to cross over into campground.

Because the slaves themselves endured much at the hands of slavery, it is not surprising that they related to the struggles and hardships endured by the Israelites before their deliverance. That they often sang about water and rivers may suggest that they believed there was a "Jordan River" that they, too, had to cross in order to reach the other shore. Many of the old Negro spirituals are based on this theme of deliverance. H.T. Burleigh's *Deep River* is no exception.

Drawing from the Bible story that depicted the deliverance of the Israelites from the bondage of Egypt, Burleigh presents the struggle for freedom by African Americans. "Deep river, my home is over Jordan." Here, spiritual life is seen as a long, hard journey. Once the river is crossed, there is a campground, or "Promised Land," where all pleasure is to be found. It's a place of peace with no more hardship or pain—Heaven.

As the children of God, the Israelites had a right to

enter their Promised Land. For the slaves, freedom from bondage also lay over the Jordan—whether it was to come in the present life or not was in God's hands. Today, believers are searching for that same place—a peaceful campground where they can rest and enjoy a "gospel feast." They long for the "other side" because it means an end to oppression and sorrow.

WADE IN THE WATER

Wade in the water
Wade in the water, children,
Wade in the water
God's a-going to trouble the water.

See that host all dressed in white,
God's a-going to trouble the water.
The leader looks like the Israelite,
God's a-going to trouble the water.

See that band all dressed in red,
God's a-going to trouble the water.
Looks like the band that Moses led,
God's a-going to trouble the water.

Look over yonder, what do you see?
God's a-going to trouble the water.
The Holy Ghost a-coming on me,
God's a-going to trouble the water.

If you don't believe I've been redeemed,
God's a-going to trouble the water.
Just follow me down to the Jordan's stream,
God's a-going to trouble the water.

Wade in the water
Wade in the water, children,
Wade in the water
God's a-going to trouble the water,

As with many of the slave songs that bore religious themes, *Wade in the Water* was one that carried a dual message for those slaves who were planning to escape. One of several used by Harriett Tubman when instructing slaves about a pending escape, the song warned those who were fleeing how to throw pursuing bloodhounds off their scent.

A powerful song with a strong and encouraging message, it seems that the main message of this popular hymn serves as a reminder of this scripture: "An angel went down at a certain season into the pool, and troubled the water: whosoever then first after the troubling of the water stepped in was made whole of whatsoever disease he had" (John 5:4). Just as the angel of the Lord had "troubled" the water to bring healing to the sick, the Lord can bring healing and deliverance to those who are oppressed.

This song was also a reminder to the escapees to travel near the rivers and streams for cover, safety, food, and direction. Like others before it, this song points directly to the Israelites, their captivity and bondage in Egypt, and their deliverance by God at the hands of Moses. The message sent by God was that Pharaoh set the Israelites free so they could worship God. To get to that place of worship, God's people had to "wade" through the waters to get to the other side and away from the pursuing armies of Pharaoh.

The Israelites crossed over on dry land because their

faith kept the waters from crashing down on them. When trouble approached in the form of their former captors, the people saw God act on their behalf. He troubled the water so that the enemy could not come near.

Trusting and believing in God leads to salvation—a relationship with God. Those who do so experience a spiritual cleansing through the "washing of water by the word" (Ephesians 5:26). The Word of God washes them clean of sin, and they step into relationship with God.

GOSPEL TRAIN

The gospel train is coming, I hear it just at hand;
I hear the car wheels moving, and rumbling through the land.

Get on board, children, get on board, children,
Get on board, children, there's room for many a more.

No signal for another train, to follow on this line;
O sinner you're forever lost, if once you're left behind.

Get on board, children, get on board, children,
Get on board, children, there's room for many a more.

She's nearing now the station, ah, sinner, don't be vain;
But come and get your ticket, be ready for the train.

Get on board, children, get on board, children,
Get on board, children, there's room for many a more.

The fare is cheap and all can go, the rich and poor are there;
No second class on board the train, no difference in the fare.

Get on board, children, get on board, children,
Get on board, children, there's room for many a more.

This train has never run off the track, she's passed through every land;
Millions and millions are on board; oh, come and join the band.

Get on board, children, get on board, children,
Get on board, children, there's room for many a more.

We soon shall reach the station, oh, how we then shall sing;
With all the heavn'ly army, we'll make the welkin ring.

Get on board, children, get on board, children,
Get on board, children, there's room for many a more.

We'll shout o'er all our sorrows, and sing forevermore,
With Christ and all his army, on that celestial shore.

"Get on board, little children" was literally an invitation to those wanting freedom to get ready because their way of escape was on the way. Though the words suggest an actual mode of transportation, it did not speak of a literal train. Rather, it spoke of the Underground Railroad, the escape system used to lead hundreds, maybe even thousands, of slaves to freedom. It was called the Underground Railroad because some of the routes the slaves took to escape were actually beneath buildings where the masters and overseers could not find them.

When Tubman, who was likened to a modern-day Moses, was on her way to the North, slaves would use such songs as *Gospel Train* and *Go Down, Moses* to spread the word. If you wanted to go or "get on board," the assurance was that there would be plenty of room—or "room for many a more."

Often, these songs were sung in church where unsuspecting masters thought the slaves had simply gathered to pray and sing songs of worship. Though their meanings are less hidden, similar messages of freedom are still conveyed today through songs sung in churches, during political protests, and even at freedom marches. With complete freedom for African Americans yet to be accomplished, there is still room for many more to get on board the freedom train.

I KNOW THE LORD'S LAID HIS HANDS ON ME

O I know the Lord, I know the Lord,
I know the Lord's laid His hands on me.
O I know the Lord, I know the Lord,
I know the Lord's laid His hands on me.
O hands on me.

Did ever you see the like before?
I know the Lord's laid His hands on me.
King Jesus preaching to the poor?
I know the Lord's laid His hands on me.

O wasn't that a happy day?
I know the Lord's laid His hands on me.
When Jesus washed my sins away.
I know the Lord's laid His hands on me.

Some seek the Lord and don't seek Him right,
I know the Lord's laid His hands on me.
They fool all day and pray at night,
I know the Lord's laid His hands on me.

My Lord's done just what He said,
I know the Lord's laid His hands on me.
He's healed the sick and raised the dead,
I know the Lord's laid His hands on me.

The slaves knew the God they served answered prayer. They believed they could sense when He touched, or "laid His hand" on them when they prayed. The

Christian slaves considered themselves bound to the words of their true Master and were fascinated by the power of healing that emanated from Jesus. However, they may not have been aware of the prophetic message in Isaiah 61:1, which declared: "The Spirit of the Lord God is upon me; because the Lord hath anointed me to preach good tidings unto the meek; he hath sent me to bind up the broken-hearted, to proclaim liberty to the captives, and the opening of the prison to them that are bound."

Nonetheless, they saw themselves as captives and saw Jesus as the One sent to them personally to bring deliverance in every way. If they were sick, their faith and prayers were the avenue by which God would come and "lay" His hands on them to bring about healing. Songs with lyrics such as "He give health unto de sick, He give sight unto de blind," give evidence that they believed God would touch them in the same manner He touched others and healed them.

For those who were subject to some infirmity, just one gesture sufficed—to touch "the hem of His garment" in imitation of the story in the Bible of the woman with the issue of blood. From then on, it would no longer be possible to feel, to cry, to walk, to talk, to sing as before. The inner self was truly transformed. The song's deep meaning still has equal application today. As faith is exercised the Lord will do for anyone what He has done for others.

MY LORD, WHAT A MORNING

My Lord, what a morning,
My Lord, what a morning,
My Lord, what a morning,
When the stars begin to fall.

You'll hear the trumpet sound,
To wake the nations underground,
Looking to my God's right hand,
When the stars begin to fall.

My Lord, what a morning,
My Lord, what a morning,
My Lord, what a morning,
When the stars begin to fall.

You'll hear the sinner mourn,
To wake the nations underground,
Looking to my God's right hand,
When the stars begin to fall.

My Lord, what a morning,
My Lord, what a morning,
My Lord, what a morning,
When the stars begin to fall.

You'll hear the Christian shout,
To wake the nations underground,
Looking to my God's right hand,
When the stars begin to fall.

My Lord, what a morning,
My Lord, what a morning,
My Lord, what a morning,
When the stars begin to fall.

With little else to occupy their mind, slaves literally took to heart every word of the Bible, committing to memory many of the words, especially those that evoked pictures of Heaven.

The opening words of this song may refer to the book of Revelation and the breaking of the sixth seal, the scene is descriptive of the end of the world.

"I beheld when he had opened the sixth seal, and, lo, there was a great earthquake; and the sun became black as sackcloth of hair, and the moon became as blood; and the stars of heaven fell unto the earth, even as a fig tree casteth her untimely figs, when she is shaken of a mighty wind" (Revelation 6:12,13).

Although the passage refers to the end of the world, quite possibly slaves viewed this passage in light of their eventual freedom from the cruel, unjust life they lived in bondage. They sang,

> *My Lord, what a morning,*
> *When the stars begin to fall.*
> *You'll hear the trumpet sound . . .*
> *You'll hear the sinner mourn . . .*
> *You'll hear the Christian shout,*
> *To wake the nations underground,*
> *Looking to my God's right hand,*
> *When the stars begin to fall.*

The drama begins in the morning, "when the stars begin to fall," and leads to the sounding of the trumpet—a victory call that indicates resurrection. It's a clarion call that is still heard today.

I WANT JESUS TO WALK WITH ME

ARRANGED BY EDWARD BOATNER

I want Jesus to walk with me,
I want Jesus to walk with me,
All along my pilgrim's journey,
Lord, I want Jesus to walk with me.

In my trials, Lord, walk with me,
In my trials, Lord, walk with me,
When my heart is almost breaking,
Lord, I want Jesus to walk with me.

When I'm in trouble, Lord, walk with me,
When I'm in trouble, Lord, walk with me,
When my head is bowed in sorrow,
Lord, I want Jesus to walk with me.

Pain and sorrow often underlined the themes of the Negro spirituals, particularly those written during the times of slavery. In this late 19th-century spiritual, composer Edward Boatner expresses what African Americans during that period must have felt.

While viewed as an obvious appeal for comfort, this "pilgrim" seeks the guidance and comfort of a loving God as he walks through a life filled with trials, tribulation, and sorrow. Slaves viewed bondage as a journey, the end of which would be deliverance to a place of freedom—the Promised Land. Their faith in God was their assurance of eventual deliverance. It gave them the courage to continue to press on.

When trials came, when trouble surrounded them, when their hearts were broken over the loss of loved ones and their heads were bowed in sorrow, God was still their friend—their deliverer. As long as He was present, walking with them, they knew everything would be all right. There are areas in life that we cannot bear alone and it is comforting to know there is a God who loves us and is always present to guide, direct, and comfort. This "song of sorrow" serves as a reminder of these things.

LET US BREAK BREAD TOGETHER

Let us break bread together on our knees (on our knees),
Let us break bread together on our knees (on our knees).
When I fall on my knees with my face to the rising sun,
O Lord, have mercy on me.

Let us drink wine together on our knees (on our knees),
Let us drink wine together on our knees (on our knees).
When I fall on my knees with my face to the rising sun,
O Lord, have mercy on me.

Let us praise God together on our knees (on our knees),
Let us praise God together on our knees (on our knees).
When I fall on my knees with my face to the rising sun,
O Lord, have mercy on me.

Another slave song embedded with a coded message, this hymn is akin to the scripture in Acts 2:42, which says, "They continued stedfastly in the apostles' doctrine and fellowship, and in breaking of bread, and in prayers." As prayer was a major part of life for the slaves, the obvious suggestion here is that the slaves sang of times when they would gather together, perhaps in the early morning or around sunrise, to pray.

The phrases "break bread together," "drink wine together," and "praise God together" suggest such a time of fellowship. But more than likely, the song signaled a clandestine meeting or gathering of some sort that would take place during that time so the slaves could discuss matters of concern—possibly a planned escape.

The song takes on a more traditional meaning today as the breaking of bread and drinking of wine symbolize the coming together of the saints to partake in open fellowship and the taking of communion.

In one of His last meals with His disciples, Jesus "took break, and blessed it, and brake it, and gave it to the disciples, and said, Take, eat; this is my body" (Matthew 26:26). A similar command followed concerning the drinking of the wine. "After the same manner also he took the cup, when he had supped, saying, This cup is the new testament in my blood: this do ye, as oft as ye drink it, in remembrance of me" (1 Corinthians 11:25).

FOLLOW THE DRINKING GOURD

Follow the drinking gourd!
Follow the drinking gourd!
For the old man is awaiting for to carry you to freedom,
If you follow the drinking gourd.

When the sun comes back and the first quail calls,
Follow the drinking gourd,
For the old man is awaiting for to carry you to freedom,
If you follow the drinking gourd.

The riverbank makes a very good road,
The dead trees will show you the way,
Left foot, peg foot traveling on,
Following the drinking gourd.

The river ends between two hills,
Follow the drinking gourd,
There's another river on the other side,
Follow the drinking gourd.

Where the great big river meets the little river,
Follow the drinking gourd,
The old man is awaiting for to carry you to freedom,
If you follow the drinking gourd

One of the most popular among the "coded" songs was *Follow the Drinking Gourd*, which is also recognized as the most famous of all slave songs. What made this coded song special was the fact that it not only carried the hidden message that an escape was imminent, but it contained a complete coded map with full details of how the escape to Canada was planned and carried out.

Slaves followed a simple direction, "Walk toward the North Star." However, unable to plan a route, they risked walking into impassable or dangerous terrain. While the North Star can sometimes be hard to recognize, the Big Dipper, which was in the northern sky and resembled a large drinking gourd, was easy to spot. Perhaps no slave song has ever been as thorough in its instructions for escape as *Follow the Drinking Gourd*.

Of all the routes out of the Deep South, this is the only one for which the details survive. In this song, the "drinking gourd" referred to the Big Dipper, a constellation close to the North Star. The choice of this constellation is obvious. During the time of slavery, many slaves fled to freedom in the North. In order to reduce the numbers of escaping slaves, owners kept slaves illiterate and totally ignorant of geography—going so far as to keep slaves from learning how to tell direction.

Members of the Underground Railroad were fully aware of the predicament of fleeing slaves. Around 1831, the Railroad began to send travelers into the South to secretly teach slaves specific routes they could navigate by using the North Star. By 1861 more than 500 abolitionists had traveled south to educate slaves about the invisible network of pathways, safe houses, and signals that were a part of the Underground Railroad. An old itinerant carpenter, known only as Peg Leg Joe, took time to give the slaves route instructions and help them to interpret the words to the song.

As soon as they were old enough to understand, even the children were taught to locate Polaris by using the stars of the Big Dipper. Estimates are that as many as 60,000 to 100,000 slaves successfully fled to freedom. *Follow the Drinking Gourd* became an instrument of instruction for escape and "The Drinking Gourd" became their symbol of freedom.

IF YE WANT TO SEE JESUS

If ye want to see Jesus, go in the wilderness,
Go in de wilderness, Go in the wilderness,
If ye want to see Jesus, Go in the wilderness,
Leaning on de Lord.

Oh, brother how do you feel, when ye come out the wilderness,
Come out de wilderness, come out the wilderness?
Oh, brother how do you feel, when ye come out the wilderness,
Leaning on de Lord?

I felt so happy when I, come out the wilderness,
Come out de wilderness, come out the wilderness.
I felt so happy when I, come out the wilderness,
Leaning on de Lord.

Oh, leaning on the Lord,
Leaning on the Lord,
Oh leaning upon the Lamb of God,
Who was slain on Calvary.

I shouted Hallelujah, when I come out the wilderness,
Come out de wilderness, come out the wilderness.
I shouted hallelujah when I, come out the wilderness,
Leaning on de Lord.

I heard the angels singing when I, come out the wilderness,
Come out de wilderness, come out the wilderness.
I heard the angels singing when I, come out the wilderness,
Leaning on de Lord.

I heard the harps a harping when I, come out the wilderness,
Come out de wilderness, come out the wilderness.
I heard the harps a harping when I, come out the wilderness,
Leaning on de Lord.

I gave the devil a battle when I, come out the wilderness,
Come out de wilderness, come out the wilderness.
I gave the devil a battle when I, come out the wilderness,
Leaning on de Lord.

Without educational skills, the slaves had little or no knowledge of proper English or grammar. Subsequently, the songs they sang were replete with dialect that to many would seem unintelligible.

In this song, the slaves sang of the joy they felt when they "come out the wilderness." Most likely the act is being compared to being delivered from the bondage of slavery.

That they sang songs such as this while still under the master's rule indicates their longing to be free and a constant thinking of what life would be once they were no longer held captive. It would be a time of joy, for they sang of shouting and singing. They imagined hearing music, and they envisioned doing one-on-one battle with the devil—the source of their oppression.

This song offered hope to an enslaved people who could find solace nowhere else aside from leaning on the Lord. That same hope is available today for those who would believe on the Lord Jesus Christ and receive Him as their Savior.

PART II

BEYOND ABOLITION:

BLACK RENAISSANCE— CIVIL RIGHTS MOVEMENT

Beyond Abolition: Black Renaissance / Civil Rights Movement covers the period between 1865 and 1960 and takes a look at some of the works from such noted composers as Thomas A. Dorsey, who was commonly referred to as the "father of gospel music" and was the author of such popular gospel songs as *Take My Hand, Precious Lord* and *Peace in the Valley*; Charles A. Tindley, whose popular hymns include *Nothing Between, Stand By Me,* and *We'll Understand It Better By and By*; and Lucie Campbell, the composer of numerous church songs including *He Understands; He'll Say, 'Well Done,'* and *Just to Behold His Face.*

Also included in this section is a sampling of songs from the Civil Rights Movement of the 1960s, including *We Shall Overcome*, a victory song based on Tindley's 1901 song *I'll Overcome Someday*, and James Weldon Johnson's popular *Lift Every Voice and Sing*. Written in 1900, this song became the victory cry of black Americans across the nation and was aptly titled "The Negro National Anthem."

PRECIOUS LORD, TAKE MY HAND

THOMAS A. DORSEY

Precious Lord, take my hand,
Lead me on, let me stand,
I am tired, I am weak, I am worn;
Through the storm, through the night,
Lead me on to the light:
Take my hand, precious Lord,
Lead me home.

When my way grows drear,
Precious Lord, linger near,
When my life is almost gone,
Hear my cry, hear my call,
Hold my hand lest I fall:
Take my hand, precious Lord,
Lead me home.

When the darkness appears
And the night draws near,
And the day is past and gone,
At the river I stand,
Guide my feet, hold my hand:
Take my hand, precious Lord,
Lead me home.

"God, You aren't worth a dime to me right now!"

It seems odd that such faithless words would come from the lips of one of the world's most renowned gospel artists. But they were the sentiments of Thomas A. Dorsey in 1932 when the man most recognized as the "father of gospel music" first learned of the tragic deaths of his wife, Nettie, and his infant son.

Dorsey grew up in Georgia no stranger to God or the Bible; in fact, his father was a preacher. Despite his life-long career in music, Dorsey was not always centered on gospel music. Dorsey enjoyed a successful career writing jazz and blues for a while. After several brushes with death, Dorsey returned to his roots, writing gospel music and singing in church.

While at a revival in St. Louis, Missouri, Dorsey received a telegram announcing that his wife and son had been killed in an accident. Stunned and grief-stricken, Dorsey lashed out at God in anger. He then turned to the only One who could relieve his hurt and pain and made a simple plea.

In his darkest hours, Dorsey asked his Lord to lead him "through the storm" and "through the night." In the weeks that followed, Dorsey put those words to music in a song he eventually called *Precious Lord, Take My Hand.* Through the leading of God, Dorsey went on to write more than 250 gospel songs, many of which have become tradition among church choirs.

"My business is to try to bring people to Christ instead of leaving them where they are," Dorsey later commented. "I write for all of God's people. All people are my people. What I share with people is love. I try to lift their spirits and let them know that God still loves them. He's still saving, and He can still give that power."[6]

This inspiring song still brings comfort to many who, like Dorsey, have run head-on into darkness and cannot find their way out. It beckons all who hear it to cast their cares on Him who loves them and will give them peace.

JUST A CLOSER WALK WITH THEE

KENNETH MORRIS, 1940

I am weak, but Thou art strong;
Jesus, keep me from all wrong;
I'll be satisfied as long
As I walk, let me walk close to Thee.

Just a closer walk with Thee,
Grant it, Jesus, is my plea,
Daily walking close to Thee,
Let it be, dear Lord, let it be.

When my feeble life is o'er,
Time for me will be no more;
Guide me gently, safely o'er
To Thy kingdom shore, to Thy shore.

Just a closer walk with Thee,
Grant it, Jesus, is my plea,
Daily walking close to Thee,
Let it be, dear Lord, let it be.

Composer Kenneth Morris wasn't sure what to expect when he rearranged a short little tune he had heard in 1940, adding verses and harmony and then publishing the song. But almost instantly Just a Closer Walk with Thee swept the nation, becoming one of the most popular gospel songs of all time.

A song of praise and adoration, this song of unknown origins signified a personal plea to the Lord for strength and comfort in a time of weakness. Though it was the song itself that, according to Morris, "put us on the map," this tune created much controversy because of questions about its authorship.

"That was not my original song," Morris would later explain in an interview in 1987, adding that he had heard it sung by a choir in Kansas City, Missouri. When he asked the choir director where the song came from, Morris recalled that the director did not know.

"It was a plantation song, and I heard it and liked it so well that I came and made an arrangement of it," said Morris. Unfortunately, Morris did not protect the song he had so diligently arranged.

"There was a Southern white publisher named Winsett, and he wanted to put it in his book. When he found out that the song had not been copyrighted, he was free to take out a copyright on it. He did not change the arrangement—not too much. He put it in sharp notes, that's the only thing he did. We didn't know too much about copyright during those days, . . . You have to remember that we didn't have any business sense at all. We knew nothing about business. We knew nothing about copyrighting or any of that end of it."[7]

"When they took my song, *Just a Closer Walk with Thee,* that woke me up. From that time on, we started to copyright our material."[8]

Despite the controversy about its origins, the song still signals a message of comfort for those who are weak or distressed. Jesus, the Comforter, is present and always ready to walk with us.

STAND BY ME

CHARLES A. TINDLEY, 1916

When the storms of life are raging,
Stand by me (stand by me);
When the storms of life are raging,
Stand by me (stand by me);
When the world is tossing me
Like a ship upon the sea
Thou Who rulest wind and water,
Stand by me (stand by me).

In the midst of tribulation,
Stand by me (stand by me);
In the midst of tribulation,
Stand by me (stand by me);
When the hosts of hell assail,
And my strength begins to fail,
Thou Who never lost a battle,
Stand by me (stand by me).
In the midst of faults and failures,
Stand by me (stand by me);

In the midst of faults and failures,
Stand by me (stand by me);
When I do the best I can,
And my friends misunderstand,
Thou Who knowest all about me,
Stand by me (stand by me).

In the midst of persecution,
Stand by me (stand by me);
In the midst of persecution,
Stand by me (stand by me);

When my foes in battle array
Undertake to stop my way,
Thou Who savèd Paul and Silas,
Stand by me (stand by me).

When I'm growing old and feeble,
Stand by me (stand by me);
When I'm growing old and feeble,
Stand by me (stand by me);
When my life becomes a burden,
And I'm nearing chilly Jordan,
O Thou "Lily of the Valley,"
Stand by me (stand by me).

There is a recurring theme in the songs and sermons of Charles A. Tindley—a belief that true change or release from worldly bondage could be attained only through struggle, similar to the struggle of going through a storm or a disastrous fire.

African Americans of that day who saw no way out of the bondage and suffering of slavery and persecution could easily relate. In most cases, they were willing to endure suffering because of their hope for a better day—on the other side. In the midst of the storm, they knew that God would be there, standing by them.

That theme is clearly portrayed in *Stand By Me*, where Tindley introduces struggle through the presence of a storm that he readily admits he cannot overcome through his own power. The plea is that God, who rules the wind and water that make up the storm, would stand by him and carry him safely through.

In a sermon he preached in 1932, titled "The Furnace of Affliction," Tindley encouraged his listeners to go willingly through the furnace in order to find a space free of the heat of persecution. It was God's way of purification, Tindley said.

"I welcome this morning all the persecutions, unkindnesses, hard sayings, and whatever God allows to come upon me. I welcome the hottest fire of trials if it is needed for my purification. Oh, the things that we have in our lives that can never go in Heaven are more numerous than we are apt to think. They must all be taken out before we leave this world. God's way to get them out may be the way of the furnace."[9]

The message of this song had a great influence among African Americans, whose daily struggles were likened to torrential storms. Songs like this encouraged listeners that the God who never lost a battle would be there to bring them through their personal storm. The cry is the same today. The storms of life still rage—through terrorism, sickness, disease, and poverty. But God's promise remains the same: "I will never leave thee, nor forsake thee" (Hebrews 13:5).

SOMETHING WITHIN

LUCIE E. CAMPBELL, 1919

Preachers and teachers would make their appeal,
Fighting as soldiers on great battlefields;
When to their pleadings, my poor heart did yield,
All I could say, there is something within.

Something within me that holdeth the reins,
Something within me that banishes pain;
Something within me I cannot explain,
All that I know, there is something within.

Have you that something, that burning desire?
Have you that something, that never doth tire?
Oh, if you have it, that Heavenly fire;
Then let the world know, there is something within.

Something within me that holdeth the reins,
Something within me that banishes pain;
Something within me I cannot explain,
All that I know, there is something within.

Lucie E. Campbell witnessed a strong faith in God and a determination not to compromise and was prompted to write this popular hymn in 1919—the first to be composed and published by an African-American woman.

A public schoolteacher for over 50 years, Campbell saw her music as her "avocation." Her songs were popular among churchgoers primarily because her lyrics related to and reflected black experiences.

The idea for *Something Within*, for example, was inspired by Connie M. Rosemond, a young blind man Campbell encountered in Memphis, Tennessee. One day Rosemond was playing hymns and spirituals on his guitar in Beale Street when some men came out of a bar and asked him to play some southern blues. The men offered to pay Rosemond five dollars for playing the music. They figured the young man was so down on his luck that he would do anything to earn some money.

Shopping at a nearby fish market, Campbell overheard the exchange and watched as a crowd gathered. She listened as Rosemond responded, "No, I can't sing the blues for you or anybody else for five dollars or fifty dollars. I'm trying to be a Christian in this dark world, and I believe I've found the way out of darkness into light. I can't explain it, but there's something within me."[10]

Those words inspired Campbell to write the song *Something Within*, which was later performed by Rosemond at the National Baptist Convention in 1919. With the pressures of temptation and compromise that surround us today, these lyrics still speak life to us. There is something within—the very presence of the Almighty God—that gives us the strength to withstand the struggles of life.

WE'LL UNDERSTAND IT BETTER BY AND BY

CHARLES A. TINDLEY

We are tossed and driv'n on the restless sea of time;
Somber skies and howling tempests oft succeed a bright sunshine;
In that land of perfect day, when the mists have rolled away,
We will understand it better by and by.
By and by, when the morning comes,
When the saints of God are gathered home,
We'll tell the story how we've overcome,
For we'll understand it better by and by.

We are often destitute of the things that life demands,
Want of food and want of shelter, thirsty hills and barren lands;
We are trusting in the Lord, and according to God's Word,
We will understand it better by and by.
By and by, when the morning comes,
When the saints of God are gathered home,
We'll tell the story how we've overcome,
For we'll understand it better by and by.

Trials dark on every hand, and we cannot understand
All the ways that God could lead us to that blessèd promised land;
But He guides us with His eye, and we'll follow till we die,
For we'll understand it better by and by.
By and by, when the morning comes,
When the saints of God are gathered home,
We'll tell the story how we've overcome,
For we'll understand it better by and by.

Temptations, hidden snares often take us unawares,
And our hearts are made to bleed for a thoughtless word or deed;
And we wonder why the test when we try to do our best,
But we'll understand it better by and by.

By and by, when the morning comes,
When the saints of God are gathered home,
We'll tell the story how we've overcome,
For we'll understand it better by and by.

The story of the African-American spirituals and hymns is more than a story of history. It is about lives lived in the face of a very difficult struggle for survival. Like many others, *We'll Understand It Better By and By* tells of a people without hope and without understanding. But these same people emerged from those trials with faith that someday they would overcome.

Like many of his songs, this one lists the many struggles and trials that Charles A. Tindley felt were necessary if there were to be any real and lasting change in one's life. This concept was widely accepted in the black community because struggle was the norm. In part of the lyrics from this hymn, "We'll tell the story of how we overcome," Tindley signals victory. The words rally those who have been through the fire, weathered the storm, waged war—and won. They thought they understood it then. Now, they understand it better.

Much of the hardship Tindley wrote about still exists today. Yet now, as then, African-American Christians trust in the Lord and His Word to guide them to the Promised Land. "All that I know now is partial and incomplete, but then I will know everything completely, just as God knows me now" (1 Corinthians 13:12 NLT).

YES, GOD IS REAL

KENNETH MORRIS, 1944

There are some things, I may not know.
There are some places I can't go.
But I am sure, of this one thing,
My God is real, for I can feel Him deep within.

My God is real, real in my soul,
My God is real, for He has washed and made me whole.
His love for me, is like pure gold,
My God is real, for I can feel Him in my soul.

Some folk may doubt, some folk may scorn,
All can desert, and leave me alone.
But as for me, I'll take God's part,
My God is real, for I can feel Him in my heart.

My God is real, real in my soul,
My God is real, for He has washed and made me whole.
His love for me, is like pure gold,
My God is real, for I can feel Him in my soul.

I cannot tell, just how I felt
When Jesus took my sins away.
But since that day, yes since that hour,
My God has been real, for I can feel His holy power.

My God is real, real in my soul,
My God is real, for He has washed and made me whole.
His love for me, is like pure gold,
My God is real, for I can feel Him in my soul.

Both doubt and skepticism may have a major influence on man when it comes to explaining or understanding the unknown—particularly in light of disastrous events and circumstances that take place on a daily basis. Music composer and publisher Kenneth Morris may have had this in mind when he answered the question that many have asked throughout the years: "Is there a God?"

A prolific and gifted composer, the New York native began his career as a jazz musician—studying his trade by day at the Manhattan Conservatory of Music and practicing it by night before enthusiastic crowds in hotels, restaurants, and lounges. Years later Morris, returning to full-time work after he was forced to the sidelines by illness that threatened his life, would abandon jazz for gospel music.

His first effort was as an arranger with a music house, where he arranged three songs that became gospel music standards: *God Shall Wipe All Tears Away* (1935), *God's Gonna Separate the Wheat from the Tare* (1937), and *I Am Sending My Timber Up to Heaven* (1939). Morris's career began to blossom in 1940 when he teamed with composer Sallie Martin and opened the Martin and Morris Music Studio.

Morris' song *Just a Closer Walk with Thee*, released in 1944, was what "put us on the map," Morris explained in a 1987 interview.[11] But it was *Yes, God Is Real*, released that same year, which would become the composer's most successful commercial composition.

Perhaps drawing from his own life experiences, Morris uses the opening lines of this tune to acknowledge that mortal man does not have all the answers to life's many situations: "There are some things I may not know. There are some places I can't go." The composer then goes straight to the core of reality in declaring and confirming the existence of a true and living God who knows all things, "But I am sure, of this one thing, My God is real, for I can feel Him deep within."

As in Morris' day, life continues to be filled with questions—many of which may never be answered. But those who have experienced God will never question His existence.

SOMETIMES I FEEL LIKE A MOTHERLESS CHILD

J. W. JOHNSON, 1926

Sometimes I feel like a motherless child,
Sometimes I feel like a motherless child,
Sometimes I feel like a motherless child.
A long ways from home,
A long ways from home.
True believer,
A long ways from home,
A long ways from home.

Sometimes I feel like I'm almost gone,
Sometimes I feel like I'm almost gone,
Sometimes I feel like I'm almost gone.
Way up in the heavenly land,
Way up in the heavenly land.
True believer,
Way up in the heavenly land,
Way up in the heavenly land.

Sometimes I feel like a motherless child,
Sometimes I feel like a motherless child,
Sometimes I feel like a motherless child.
There's praying everywhere,
There's praying everywhere.
True believer,
There's praying everywhere,
There's praying everywhere.

Writer, poet, songwriter, and distinguished statesman James Weldon Johnson could not have been thinking of himself when he wrote this touching melody. Unlike the thousands of slave children he had read about, Johnson never knew the pain of being sold and separated from his parents.

He and his brother, J. Rosamond Johnson, were raised by their natural parents and did not experience slavery. Their father was the head waiter at a resort hotel in Jacksonville, Florida, and their mother, born in the Bahamas and educated in New York City, was the first black woman to teach in a public school in Florida. Both parents were also very talented musically.

Johnson's obvious inspiration for such a reflective song had to be the history of those who had come before him—those slave children who were taken away from their parents at an early age and sold on the auction block. During the time of slavery, safety was a rarity for black children. Every black mother lived with the fear that her child could be taken at any time. More often than not, that was the case. Like cattle, children were torn away from their families, sold at auction, and shipped off to strange lands—never to see their families again. Many times, children were transported to other states, far away from family and, as Johnson points out, "a long ways from home."

Through this spiritual, Johnson expresses the pain and agony of a child taken from his mother. There may not have been a natural comfort during such times, but there was a hope—a hope that someday they would be reunited "Way up in the Heavenly land."

THE STORM IS PASSING OVER

O courage, my soul, and let us journey on,
For tho' the night is dark, it won't be very long.
O thanks be to God, the morning light appears,
And the storm is passing over, Hallelujah!

> *Hallelujah! Hallelujah!*
> *The storm is passing over,*
> *Hallelujah!*

O billows rolling high, and thunder shakes the ground,
The lightnings flash, and tempest all around,
But Jesus walks the sea and calms the angry waves,
And the storm is passing over, Hallelujah!

> *Hallelujah! Hallelujah!*
> *The storm is passing over,*
> *Hallelujah!*

The stars have disappeared, and distant lights are dim,
My soul is filled with fears, the seas are breaking in.
I hear the Master cry, "Be not afraid, 'tis I,"
And the storm is passing over, Hallelujah!

> *Hallelujah! Hallelujah!*
> *The storm is passing over,*
> *Hallelujah!*

Now soon we shall reach the distant shining shore,
Then free from all the storms, we'll rest forevermore.
And safe within the veil, we'll furl the river sail,
And the storm will all be over, Hallelujah!

> *Hallelujah! Hallelujah!*
> *The storm is passing over,*
> *Hallelujah!*

During an era when he not only witnessed but experienced hardship in many ways, it was easy for Charles Tindley to write about the subjects in his songs. Judging from the theme that emerged from much of his music and sermons, Tindley believed that release from worldly bondage could be attained only through struggle and endurance. The object of that release, obviously, was the God that he so strongly believed in.

Often, Tindley related the struggles blacks encountered to the rage and torment experienced in a storm. In the song, *Stand By Me*, for instance, lyrics such as "When the world is tossing me like a ship upon the sea" might have described the way slaves were exchanged and sold—a feeling of being "tossed" from one master to the next.

The Storm Is Passing Over suggests the need to withstand the hurt and pain such dealings cause, realizing the promise of victory is on the other side:

> *Now soon we shall reach the distant shining shore,*
> *Then free from all the storms, we'll rest forevermore.*

The comfort blacks found through the words of such songs still brings peace today as the busyness of everyday life deals hardship and trouble on every hand. God still promises that He will calm our storms with the words "Peace, be still!"

LET JESUS FIX IT FOR YOU

If your life, in days gone by
Has not been good and true,
In your way no longer try,
But let Him fix it for you.

Perhaps your temper is to blame
For many wrongs you do,
Take it to God in Jesus' name;
And He will fix it for you.

If, in your home, the trouble is
The course you should pursue,
Go talk with God, your hand in His
And He will fix it for you.

And if some sin your soul has bound
With cords you cannot undo,
At Jesus' feet, go lay it down
And He will fix it for you.

Maybe to you the world is dark,
And comforts far and few.
Let Jesus own and rule your heart,
And He will fix it for you.

Let Jesus fix it for you,
He knows just what to do.
Whenever you pray, let Him have His way,
And He will fix it for you.

When it came to writing songs, few composers were better than Charles A. Tindley. When it came to preaching the gospel, this black Methodist minister, often referred to as the "prince of preachers," was in a class by himself. As the founder of one of the largest Methodist congregations serving the African-American community on the East Coast, Tindley often used his personal experience of escaping slavery and poverty to convey certain messages in his sermons and hymns.

The Reverend Henry Nichols recalled that Tindley's hymns "came out of a rich personal experience, and then it became meaningful to us who were born during or before the Depression."[12] *Let Jesus Fix It for You*, like many of Tindley's songs, came from ordinary experiences in his ministry.

Nichols recalled that as a young boy he would volunteer to assist in soup lines Tindley had established to feed hungry people. "There'd be lines for blocks waiting to get a little soup," said Nichols. "And then he'd [Tindley] give them soup and sit down and talk to them about their soul."[13] Nichols also recalled the words Tindley once spoke to a group of people that echoed the message from his hymn, *Let Jesus Fix It for You*:

"You know, the only way you can really become defeated on your way to heaven is to allow life's difficulties to get inside of you, and to turn you sour. One of the things that we have to do—we must do—is to make sure that we do not try to take vengeance. That if we belong to Him, then He in His own time will take care of the situation."[14]

Submission, trust, and faith are key elements of this great Tindley hymn, which is still heard in churches today. Tindley recognized what still needs to be acknowledged today—that God, who is limitless, is able to fix any situation. We need only trust Him to do so, and then give our problems over to Him.

HE UNDERSTANDS; HE'LL SAY, 'WELL DONE'

LUCIE CAMPBELL

If when you give the best of your service,
Telling the world that the Savior is come.
Be not dismayed if men don't believe you,
He understands; He'll say, "Well done."

Oh, when I come to the end of my journey,
Wearied of life and the battle is won.
Carrying the staff and the cross of redemption,
He understands; He'll say, "Well done."

In some form or another, controversy has always been a part of the church. Lucie Campbell experienced more than her share of controversy and heartbreak during years of church service, even to the point of once being thrown out of the Metropolitan Baptist Church where she and her mother had been long-standing members. It was such an occasion that led to Campbell's writing of this hymn which, rather than suggesting anger or bitterness, translates the thought of misunderstanding.

The situation began in 1922, when a dispute arose at Metropolitan over a replacement for the pastor who had resigned. The person chosen by the congregation did not meet with Campbell's approval. "There was much joy in the congregation as it awaited the arrival of its new pastor," the Reverend Charles Walker later wrote in an account of the incident. "Joy in all quarters except among the followers of Miss Lucie. Unofficial meetings were called at Miss Lucie's home to discuss the strategy to prevent him from assuming the pastorate, and Miss Lucie was the leader of the opposition . . . . Miss Lucie was a woman of considerable power and influence."[15]

Tensions began to mount the day the new pastor was to arrive and preach his first sermon at Metropolitan. Shortly before his arrival, Campbell had decided that a minister of her choosing should preach and had instructed him to conduct the service. In addition, members of the now-divided choir—those who had chosen to side with Campbell—had taken over the choir stand. Campbell was at the piano.

Before long, members began to protest. When Campbell was asked to leave, "she became infuriated, took her umbrella…and the congregation exploded!" Walker wrote.

Fights broke out, and the police were summoned to quell the dangerous situation.

"It was reported that the next evening the deacons met and voted to church Miss Lucie and all her followers. When a member of a congregation is churched, he or she is brought into what is like the trial that precedes what the Catholic church calls excommunication. So they voted to church Miss Lucie . . . . This recommendation was brought to the church in a subsequent church meeting, and the vote was placed before the church body. It was passed by a majority vote that the right hand of fellowship be withdrawn from those members involved in this disturbance. Miss Lucie, along with about one hundred of her followers, were put out of the Metropolitan Baptist Church."[16]

Shocked by the decision, Campbell left the church, never to return. Reportedly, Campbell remained "churchless" for years as she was barred from other churches by pastors who had heard about the incident. "Her pain was intense. Her embarrassment was penetrating. Her sorrow was inexpressible," Walker wrote. "This perhaps would not have been so if she could have shaken the idea that she was misunderstood. However, out of the milieu of that awful experience, Lucie Campbell composed one of her most inspiring gospel hymns."[17]

JUST TO BEHOLD HIS FACE

LUCIE CAMPBELL

Not just to kneel with the angels,
Nor to see loved ones who've gone.
Not just to drink at the fountain,
Under the great white throne.

Just to behold His face,
Yes, just to behold His face;
All I will want up in heaven,
Is just to behold His face.

Not just to join in the chorus,
And sing with those that are blessed.
And bathe my soul that is weary,
In the sea of heavenly rest.

But I'll look for the One who saved me,
From a death of sin and disgrace.
What joy when I get up in heaven,
Just to behold His face.

Just to behold His face,
Yes, just to behold His face;
All I will want up in heaven,
Is just to behold His face.

Yes, I want to see Jesus,
Who bore His cross in my stead.
Who willingly suffered affliction,
With a crown of thorns on His head.

Precious Fount that was opened on Calvary,
For me—what amazing Grace.
What joy will be mine forever,
Just to behold His face.

Just to behold His face,
Yes, just to behold His face;
All I will want up in heaven,
Is just to behold His face.

I'll bless the hand that guided,
I'll bless the heart that planned.
I'll not rest until I see Jesus,
And He takes me by the hand.
Father, mother, sister and brother,
And all who have won this race.
Will be there to join in that chorus,
As we all shall behold His face.

Just to behold His face,
Yes, just to behold His face;
All I will want up in heaven,
Is just to behold His face.

Church controversy for Lucie Campbell did not end with her dramatic experience at the Metropolitan Baptist Church. Years later, there was to be yet another major confrontation at the Central Baptist Church, where Campbell served as the choir director. Again, the controversy would lead to Campbell's expulsion from the church and the eventual writing of another hymn.

A member of the Central Baptist Church, whose name

is not recorded in history, recalled the incident that led up to Campbell's expulsion this way:

"In 1929, I was a member of the Junior Choir . . . . It was our responsibility to sing the second and fourth Sundays in each month. Miss Campbell directed the Adult Choir, which sang on the first and third Sundays.

"One fourth Sunday, some important out-of-town guests came, and Miss Campbell wanted the Adult Choir to sing instead of the Junior Choir. The Junior Choir refused to leave the choir stand, and some strong words were exchanged. A church meeting was called to deal with the problem . . . . When the meeting was opened and the matter brought to the floor, one young person asked if it was lawful for a nonmember to be present in this meeting. The reason for the question was that Miss Lucie was not a member of Central Baptist Church, even though she directed the choir.

"When the young woman raised the question of membership, Miss Lucie yelled out, 'I pay as much money in this church as anybody!' The young people retorted, 'It doesn't matter how much money you give to the church. That does not make you a member.'"[18]

The church sided with the junior choir, and the matter was closed. Campbell was later received into the church as a member, but controversy was far from over for her. In 1943, more problems surfaced when Campbell informed her pastor of problems she was having with one of the church deacons and said she refused to work with the man. Following a meeting with Campbell, the pastor asked her to apologize to the deacon. Campbell refused. A church meeting was called, the facts presented, and again Campbell was asked to apologize. Again, she refused. This time, the members chose to expel her from the church.

The following Sunday, Campbell returned to church and sat in the congregation. When the invitation was given, she went forth to be received back into the church. Her pastor ignored her presence. Campbell returned to her seat but was later escorted out of the church by police, who had been called by one of the deacons. Campbell later sued the church and its pastor, but a judge threw the case out of court.

Reflecting on the experience, Campbell considered her life and the struggles she had faced in her efforts to serve her God. Out of that came the song *Just to Behold His Face,* which bore a strong message of commitment that served to encourage others and Campbell as well.

The message is still the same. We don't work in the church for what we can get back, but to please God. It is Him we desire to please—not man, and not ourselves.

LEAVE IT THERE

CHARLES A. TINDLEY, 1916

If the world from you withhold of its silver and its gold,
And you have to get along with meager fare,
Just remember, in His Word, how He feeds the little bird;
Take your burden to the Lord and leave it there.
Leave it there, leave it there,
Take your burden to the Lord and leave it there.
If you trust and never doubt, He will surely bring you out.
Take your burden to the Lord and leave it there.

If your body suffers pain and your health you can't regain,
And your soul is almost sinking in despair,
Jesus knows the pain you feel, He can save and He can heal;
Take your burden to the Lord and leave it there.
Leave it there, leave it there,
Take your burden to the Lord and leave it there.
If you trust and never doubt, He will surely bring you out.
Take your burden to the Lord and leave it there.

When your enemies assail and your heart begins to fail,
Don't forget that God in heaven answers prayer;
He will make a way for you and will lead you safely through.
Take your burden to the Lord and leave it there.
Leave it there, leave it there,
Take your burden to the Lord and leave it there.
If you trust and never doubt, He will surely bring you out.
Take your burden to the Lord and leave it there.

When your youthful days are gone and old age is stealing on,
And your body bends beneath the weight of care;
He will never leave you then, He'll go with you to the end.
Take your burden to the Lord and leave it there.
Leave it there, leave it there,

Take your burden to the Lord and leave it there.
If you trust and never doubt, He will surely bring you out.
Take your burden to the Lord and leave it there.

When a man who was a constant worrier went to Charles A. Tindley for advice in dealing with his problems, the popular Methodist minister looked at him with concern and offered the following instruction, "My advice to you is put all your troubles in a sack, take them to the Lord, and leave them there."

Shortly after that, Tindley was inspired to write a song based on that same piece of advice. *Leave It There* became one of the most popular spiritual hymns of all time. The lyrics, loosely based on Psalm 55:22, send an invitation to any who are burdened to "Cast your cares upon the Lord and He will sustain you."

"Why art though cast down, O my soul? . . . hope thou in God: for I shall yet praise him for the help of his countenance:"(Psalm 42.5). Tindley's timely message still rings clear today.

NOTHING BETWEEN

CHARLES A. TINDLEY

Nothing between my soul and my Savior,
Naught of this world's delusive dream;
I have renounced all sinful pleasure;
Jesus is mine, there's nothing between.

Nothing between, like worldly pleasure;
Habits of life, though harmless they seem;
Must not my heart from Him ever sever;
He is my all, there's nothing between.

Nothing between, like pride or station;
Self or friends shall not intervene;
Though it may cost me much tribulation,
I am resolved, there's nothing between.

Nothing between, e'en many hard trials,
Though the whole world against me convene;
Watching with prayer and much self denial,
I'll triumph at last, there's nothing between.

Charles A. Tindley was busy working on a sermon one day when a strong gust of wind blew through his study, rustling the papers he was working with. Now, now, Tindley thought, let nothing between. Out of that single thought came one of Tindley's best loved hymns, *Nothing Between*.

What is it that comes between you and your worship to God? Maybe it's your job. Or perhaps it is a hobby.

Whatever it is, it is not worth sacrificing the relationship God has established between himself and you.

Reflective of the scripture that says nothing "shall be able to separate us from the love of God" (Romans 8:39), this song reminds us of our close relationship with our Heavenly Father. That relationship is so strong, the commitment so strong, we cannot help but echo the words that proclaim, "I have renounced all sinful pleasure; Jesus is mine, there's nothing between."

OH, HAPPY DAY

Oh happy day (Oh happy day)
Oh happy day (Oh happy day)
When Jesus washed (when Jesus washed)
When Jesus washed (when Jesus washed)
When Jesus washed (when Jesus washed)
He washed my sins away (Oh happy day)
Oh happy day (Oh happy day)

He taught me how to watch, fight, and pray
Fight and pray
And live rejoicing every, every day,
Every day.

Oh happy day (Oh happy day)
Oh happy day (Oh happy day)
When Jesus washed (when Jesus washed)
When Jesus washed (when Jesus washed)
When Jesus washed (when Jesus washed)
He washed my sins away (Oh happy day)
Oh happy day (Oh happy day)

During the late 1960s gospel music began to slowly make its way into the mainstream. Previously, the performance of such music had been limited to religious events and public venues for African-American audiences.

That quickly changed with the release of this crossover hit by the Edwin Hawkins Singers in 1968. This gospel arrangement of an older hymn is considered to be the song that opened the door for the commercial exploitation of gospel music. Containing elements of various styles of contemporary black music, the song was categorized as gospel and soul music on many black radio stations. Simultaneously *Oh, Happy Day* was played as "pop" music on some of the Top 40 stations.

Unsure as to how to label the popular song, one radio disk jockey once introduced it this way, "It sounds like gospel and it sounds like soul. Whatever it is, the beat has a groove. I like it and I'm gonna play it."[19]

Oh, Happy Day raised the bar, which today has been raised even higher, as more and more contemporary gospel artist are melding pop, soul, and gospel to communicate the simple message of God's love. It is a song of deliverance that still echoes the sentiments of the many who, even today, have longed for freedom and realized it through a loving Savior.

MARCHING 'ROUND SELMA

Marching 'round Selma like Jericho,
Jericho, Jericho.
Marching 'round Selma like Jericho
For segregation wall must fall
Look at people answering
To the Freedom Fighters call
Black, Brown, and White Americans say
Segregation must fall
Good evening freedom's fighters
Tell me where you're bound
Tell me where you're marching
From Selma to Montgomery town

The Negro spiritual has always played an important role in the cry of black people who sought their freedom. Often, the words of some of those traditional songs were changed to adapt to certain situations. For example, during the Civil Rights Movement in Alabama, the words to *Joshua Fit the Battle of Jerico* were rearranged slightly to become a new freedom song titled *Marching 'Round Selma*.

This particular song may have had a direct relationship to the Selma-to-Montgomery March for voting rights, which took place in March 1965 in Alabama. On March 7, a day now referred to as "Bloody Sunday," about 600 civil rights marchers headed east out of Selma on U.S. Route 80 to Montgomery. When they reached the Edmund Pettus Bridge, the group was attacked by state and local law enforcement officers who used clubs and tear gas to drive them back to Selma.

The attack was televised and by the time Dr. Martin Luther King Jr. led a second "symbolic" march to the bridge two days later, whites and blacks from other parts of the country had joined in their struggle. The group prayed, turned around and returned to Selma. Then civil rights leaders sought and obtained court protection for a march from Selma to the state capitol in Montgomery. On Sunday, March 21, about 3,200 marchers set out for Montgomery, walking 12 miles a day and sleeping in fields. By the time they reached the capitol on Thursday, March 25, the group had grown to 25,000. Less than five months after the last of the three marches, President Lyndon Johnson signed the Voting Rights Act of 1965.

I SHALL NOT BE MOVED

I shall not be moved.
Like a tree planted by the water,
I shall not be moved.
When my cross is heavy,
I shall not be moved.
Like a tree planted by the water,
I shall not be moved.

The church of God is marching . . .
I shall not be moved.
Like a tree planted by the water,
I shall not be moved.

King Jesus is our captain . . .
I shall not be moved.
Like a tree planted by the water,
I shall not be moved.

Come and join the army . . .
I shall not be moved.
Like a tree planted by the water,
I shall not be moved.

Fighting sin and Satan . . .
I shall not be moved,
Like a tree planted by the water.
I shall not be moved.

When my burden's heavy . . .
I shall not be moved.
Like a tree planted by the water,
I shall not be moved.

Don't let the world deceive you . . .
I shall not be moved.
Like a tree planted by the water,
I shall not be moved.

If my friends forsake me . . .
I shall not be moved.
Like a tree planted by the water,
I shall not be moved.

God has promised many blessings to His children—
those who believe on Him and call Him Lord. Perhaps no
one has exhibited this belief as much as those held in the
bonds of slavery. Many slaves, though poorly educated,
spent abundant time with God—reading His Word, praying, and singing the songs of deliverance.

If there was one priority with them as slaves, it was that
they not lose their identity—that they never allow their per-
sonality to dissolve under the lashes of the master. Where
violence reigned, those held in captivity would try to intro-
duce conscience. They did not want to gain Heaven before
fulfilling their duty on earth. They were much like the
description of Joshua in another old Negro spiritual, *Lit'le
David,* who "never would quit 'till his work was done."

As seen in the previous entry, a similar stance is taken
today by African Americans intent on fighting for civil
rights. Even today, when civil rights issues still arise, the
battle cry remains the same: "We shall not be moved.

WE SHALL OVERCOME

We shall overcome
We shall overcome
We shall overcome some day
Oh deep in my heart
I do believe
We shall overcome some day

We'll walk hand in hand
We'll walk hand in hand
We'll walk hand in hand some day
Oh deep in my heart
I do believe
We shall overcome some day

We shall all be free
We shall all be free
We shall all be free some day
Oh deep in my heart
I do believe
We shall overcome some day

We are not afraid
We are not afraid
We are not afraid today
Oh deep in my heart
I do believe
We shall overcome some day

We are not alone
We are not alone
We are not alone today
Oh deep in my heart

I do believe
We shall overcome some day

The whole wide world around
The whole wide world around
The whole wide world around some day
Oh deep in my heart
I do believe
We shall overcome some day

We shall overcome
We shall overcome
We shall overcome some day
Oh deep in my heart
I do believe
We shall overcome some day

Widely recognized as a protest song, *We Shall Overcome* was born out of two other well-known African-American spirituals, *I'll Overcome Someday*, written by Charles Tindley in 1900, and a 19th-century, pre-Civil War hymn titled *No More Auction Block for Me*. This popular Negro spiritual is recognized as the anthem for the American Civil Rights Movement.

There are several accounts of how *We Shall Overcome* evolved. But most accounts indicate that one of its first prominent uses as a protest song was in 1945 by a group of striking workers from the Negro Food and Tobacco Union in Charleston, South Carolina. Another account credits singer and songwriter, Pete Seeger, who collaborated with

Dr. Martin Luther King, Rosa Parks, and other civil rights activists during 1960s Civil Rights Movement.

Seeger's account:

"In 1946, several hundred employees of the American Tobacco Company in Charleston, South Carolina, were on strike. They sang on the picket line to keep up their spirits. Lucille Simmons started singing the song on the picket line and changed one important word from 'I' to 'We.' Zilphia Horton learned it when a group of strikers visited the Highland Fold School, the Labor Education Center in Tennessee. She taught it to me and we published it as *We Shall Overcome* in our songletter, 'People's Songs Bulletin.' In 1952, I taught it to Guy Carawan and Frank Hamilton. Guy introduced the song to the founding convention of SNCC (Student Nonviolent Coordinating Committee) in North Carolina.

"I started singing *We Shall Overcome* all over the country . . . . That's probably the way I sang it to Martin Luther King just six months after he won the bus boycott in 1957. . . . I sang it for the crowd. The next day, driving back to Kentucky for a speaking engagement, King said, 'We will overcome.'"[20]

Soon afterwards, the song was repeated in places around the world. Striking miners sang it in 1989, Chinese students have sung it in Tiananmen Square, and South Africans have proclaimed it in their struggle against Apartheid.

Still popular for its truth and the reality it brings to life today, the theme brought even more revelation when it echoed throughout New York's Yankee Stadium on September 23, 2001. The Harlem Boys and Girls Choir sang the song during a special ceremony honoring those who perished in the September 11, 2001, terrorist attacks.

I'LL OVERCOME SOMEDAY

CHARLES A. TINDLEY

This world is one great battlefield
With forces all arrayed,
If in my heart I do not yield
I'll overcome some day.
I'll overcome some day,
I'll overcome some day,
If in my heart I do not yield,
I'll overcome some day.

Both seen and unseen powers join
To drive my soul astray,
But with His Word a sword of mine,
I'll overcome some day.
I'll overcome some day,
I'll overcome some day,
But with His Word a sword of mine,
I'll overcome some day.

A thousand snares are set for me,
And mountains in my way,
If Jesus will my leader be,
I'll overcome some day.
I'll overcome some day,
I'll overcome some day,
If Jesus will my leader be,
I'll overcome some day.

I fail so often when I try
My Savior to obey;
It pains my heart and then I cry,
Lord, make me strong some day.

Lord, make me strong some day,
Lord, make me strong some day;
It pains my heart and then I cry,
Lord, make me strong some day.
My mind is not to do the wrong,
But walk the narrow way;
I'm praying as I journey on,
To overcome some day.
To overcome some day,
To overcome some day;
I'm praying as I journey on,
To overcome some day.

Though many a time no signs appear,
Of answer when I pray;
My Jesus says I need not fear,
He'll make it plain some day.
I'll be like Him some day,
I'll be like Him some day;
My Jesus says I need not fear,
He'll make it plain some day.

The model for the popular protest song of the 1960s, *We Shall Overcome*, was written by Charles Tindley around 1900, shortly before Tindley became pastor of the Calvary Methodist Episcopal Church in Philadelphia, Pennsylvania. It became one of his two most popular songs. The other, *Stand By Me*, was revised and became a national hit for singers Ben E. King and The Drifters.

Obviously aware of the conditions of the African Americans at this time, Tindley used their situation as a backdrop for this arresting song. The world, as slaves saw it, was one great big battlefield and all the slave masters were like giants against them.

If they were to be victorious, they could not give up.

> *This world is one great battlefield*
> *With forces all arrayed,*
> *If in my heart I do not yield*
> *I'll overcome some day.*

The message of this song is timeless, speaking to every obstacle that is common to man. "A thousand snares are set for me, and mountains in my way." But with Jesus leading and guiding, we will overcome someday.

LIFT EVERY VOICE AND SING

(THE NEGRO NATIONAL ANTHEM)

JAMES WELDON JOHNSON, 1900

Lift ev'ry voice and sing, till earth and heaven ring,
Ring with the harmonies of Liberty.
Let our rejoicing rise, high as the list'ning skies,
Let it resound loud as the rolling sea.
Sing a song full of faith that the dark past has taught us.
Sing a song full of the hope that the present has brought us.
Facing the rising sun of our new day begun,
Let us march till victory is won.
Stony the road we trod, bitter the chast'ning rod
Felt in the days when hope unborn has died.
Yet with a steady beat, have not our weary feet
Come to the place for which our fathers sighed?
We have come over a way that with tears has been watered.
We have come, treading our path thro' the blood
of the slaughtered.
Out from the gloomy past, till now we stand at last
Where the white gleam of our bright star is cast.
God of our weary years, God of our silent tears,
Thou who hast brought us thus far on the way.
Thou who hast by Thy might, led us into the light
Keep us for ever in the path, we pray.
Lest our feet stray from the places, our God, where we met Thee.
Lest our hearts, drunk with the wine of the world, we forget Thee.
Shadowed beneath Thy hand, may we for ever stand
True to our God, true to our native land.

No doubt the constant struggle of blacks to be free was in the back of his mind when noted poet, author, and educator, James Weldon Johnson, wrote a poem he titled "Lift Every Voice and Sing." Little did he know then that the poem inspired by his ancestry, when put to music, would become the victory cry of black Americans as "The Negro National Anthem."

"A group of young men in Jacksonville, Florida arranged to celebrate Lincoln's birthday in 1900," Johnson explained in his autobiography.[21] He had been asked to speak at the function. Instead, Johnson decided to write a poem, then changed his mind and asked his brother, J. Rosamond Johnson, a music teacher, to help him write a song.

Johnson recalled that while writing the words to his now famous song, "the spirit of the poem" took hold of him through two single lines near the end of the first stanza. They read: "Sing a song full of the faith that the dark past has taught us. Sing a song full of the hope that the present has brought us."

A reflection of how a strong faith in God had kept his ancestors strong during the dark period of oppression and slavery and a hope of what the future might hold were black people ever to know true freedom, possibly inspired the next two lines: "Facing the rising sun of our new day begun, let us march till victory is won."

Years later Johnson would write about that experience,

recalling how after sending the song to their publisher in New York, he and his brother thought little more about it. However, the heritage behind those words made it a song that the public could not forget. "The school children of Jacksonville kept singing it," Johnson wrote. "They went off to other schools and sang it. They became teachers and taught it to other children. Within 20 years it was sung all over the South and in some other parts of the country."[22]

In 1920, Johnson became executive secretary of the National Association for the Advancement of Colored People (NAACP), and the group adopted *Lift Every Voice and Sing* as its official song.

Taught in schools, churches, and civic organizations for decades, this powerfully inspiring song, with its message of hope and strength, remains one of the most beloved songs among African Americans.

Part III

*E*uro–American Contributors:

Hymns Embraced by the African–American Church

In addition to the contributions of slave songs, hymns, spirituals, and gospel music to the African-American church, this collection would not be complete without the contributions of a number of white composers and writers.

Among those was Dr. Isaac Watts, an English minister and physician, who in the 1600s openly expressed his view that church music as presented through hymns lacked any vibrant expression. "To see the dull indifference, the negligent and thoughtless air, that sits upon the face of the whole assembly while the psalm is on their lips, might tempt even a charitable observer to suspect the fervour of inward religion," Watts once wrote.[23]

Watts gave the church a freer, more powerful means of expressing its faith and worship through the creation of such lively hymns as *When I Survey the Wondrous Cross*, *Jesus Shall Reign*, and *Joy to the World*. His influence would soon touch the lives of other famous composers such as Charles and John Wesley, and John Newton, who adopted Watts' style.

Songs by these and others brought about a new direction in church music, moving it away from psalm singing toward religious poem singing. Since that time, church music has expanded to include the singing of the spirituals, gospels, and the modern praise songs that are so popular today.

While many of these old English hymns, penned some 250 years ago, are identified as "Negro Spirituals" or "traditional" black songs, it is interesting to note that many were, in fact, written by whites. Just as African Americans took the Christian religion as their own, they also embraced some of its music—breathing into it a new life and adapting it to their history, culture, and circumstances.

AMAZING GRACE

JOHN NEWTON, 1831

Amazing grace! How sweet the sound
That saved a wretch like me!
I once was lost, but now am found;
Was blind, but now I see.

'Twas grace that taught my heart to fear,
And grace my fears relieved;
How precious did that grace appear
The hour I first believed.

Through many dangers, toils, and snares,
I have already come;
'Tis grace hath brought me safe thus far,
And grace will lead me home.

The Lord has promised good to me,
His Word my hope secures;
He will my Shield and Portion be,
As long as life endures.

Yea, when this flesh and heart shall fail,
And mortal life shall cease,
I shall possess, within the veil,
A life of joy and peace.

The earth shall soon dissolve like snow,
The sun forbear to shine;
But God, Who called me here below,
Shall be forever mine.

When we've been there ten thousand years,
Bright shining as the sun,
We've no less days to sing God's praise
Than when we'd first begun.

In its original version, *Amazing Grace* contained 25 couplets but only 20 were published in the *New York Tribune* in 1861. The first seven are included here. The words of this powerful hymn still carry a universal appeal today. It serves as an encouragement that as God's oppressed people continue to pray and trust Him for deliverance, He will hear their cry.

The following words, inscribed on John Newton's headstone upon his death in 1807, were a testimony befitting the life of John Newton, who spent a good portion of his life captaining a crew of slave-traders:

"John Newton, clerk, once an infidel and libertine, a servant of slavers in Africa, was, by the rich mercy of our Lord and Savior Jesus Christ, preserved, restored, pardoned, and appointed to preach the Faith he had long labored to destroy."[24]

Newton himself penned the words, perhaps as a way of confirming to himself and to the world the sinful life he had lived and reaffirming the miraculous transformation that had taken place in his life at the hands of God.

At the tender age of 11, this youngster from Olney, England, went to work on his father's ship as a seaman. Newton navigated his way through jobs on several ships—working on the islands and mainland of the West African coast, collecting slaves for sale to visiting traders.

Before long, the astute young man became captain of his own ship, continuing the cruel and inhumane practice of capturing and selling Africans into slavery. In March 1748, during a particularly stormy voyage from Africa to England, Newton picked up a copy of the book *Imitation of Christ* and began to read it. The message of the book and the threatening waves surrounding him were enough to convince Newton of his spiritual needs, which prompted him to accept Jesus Christ as his personal Savior.

Despite his newfound faith, it would be years before Newton would discontinue the practice of slave trade. But eventually Newton fell under strong conviction that his work was cruel and inhumane and he became a strong crusader against slavery.

In 1764, at age 39, the Anglican Church ordained Newton and he took on his first pastorate at a small village church in Olney. He often told the story of his early life, the work he had come to despise, and the amazing conversion he experienced at the hands of God. He marveled at God's mercy and grace that had changed his life and used it as a major focus when he preached.

Along with his friend, classic literary writer William Cowper, Newton also produced the famous *Olney Hymns* hymnal, a collection of 349 hymns—many of which expressed the simple, heartfelt faith of Newton's preaching.

Among those was the hymn *Amazing Grace*.

It is no wonder that Newton was amazed at God's mercy and His grace. The words of this song were imprinted on his heart and soul. Those same words still bring a passionate understanding of the love, mercy, and grace that God generously demonstrates to His children as we reach out to Him.

COUNT YOUR BLESSINGS

JOHNSON OATMAN, JR.

When upon life's billows you are tempest tossed,
When you are discouraged, thinking all is lost,
Count your many blessings, name them one by one,
And it will surprise you what the Lord hath done.

Count your blessings, name them one by one,
Count your blessings, see what God hath done!
Count your blessings, name them one by one,
And it will surprise you what the Lord hath done.

Are you ever burdened with a load of care?
Does the cross seem heavy you are called to bear?
Count your many blessings, every doubt will fly,
And you will keep singing as the days go by.

Count your blessings, name them one by one,
Count your blessings, see what God hath done!
Count your blessings, name them one by one,
And it will surprise you what the Lord hath done.

When you look at others with their lands and gold,
Think that Christ has promised you His wealth untold;
Count your many blessings. Wealth can never buy
Your reward in heaven, nor your home on high.

Count your blessings, name them one by one,
Count your blessings, see what God hath done!
Count your blessings, name them one by one,
And it will surprise you what the Lord hath done.

So, amid the conflict whether great or small,
Do not be disheartened, God is over all;
Count your many blessings, angels will attend,
Help and comfort give you to your journey's end.

Count your blessings, name them one by one,
Count your blessings, see what God hath done!
Count your blessings, name them one by one,
And it will surprise you what the Lord hath done.

Reverend Johnson Oatman Jr., a Methodist preacher, was one of the most important and prolific gospel song-writers of the late 19th and early 20th centuries. Although there is much information available about his personal life, little has been recorded about the origin of Oatman's *Count Your Blessings*, one of the most popular hymns of his time.

History records that Oatman juggled his time between preaching, engaging in the mercantile business, and serving as an administrator for a large insurance company in New Jersey. In addition, he found time to pen more than 5,000 hymns. *Count Your Blessings*, reportedly sung in churches around the world, first appeared in a publication by Edwin O. Excell in 1897 called *Songs for Young People*.

One writer said of the acclaimed song, "Like a beam of sunlight, it has brightened up the dark places of the earth." While introducing the song during a meeting, another heralded the tune by saying, "In South London the men sing it, the boys whistle it, and the women rock their babies to sleep on this hymn."[26]

Considered to be one of the most familiar of all hymns, the song was a favorite in the early Sunday schools and is still a widely recognized favorite in many church circles today.

I MUST TELL JESUS

ELISHA A. HOFFMAN, 1893

I must tell Jesus all of my trials;
I cannot bear these burdens alone;
In my distress He kindly will help me;
He ever loves and cares for His own.
Refrain:
I must tell Jesus! I must tell Jesus!
I cannot bear my burdens alone;
I must tell Jesus! I must tell Jesus!
Jesus can help me, Jesus alone.
I must tell Jesus all of my troubles;
He is a kind, compassionate friend;
If I but ask Him, He will deliver,
Make of my troubles quickly an end.
Tempted and tried, I need a great Savior;
One Who can help my burdens to bear;
I must tell Jesus, I must tell Jesus;
He all my cares and sorrows will share.
Refrain
O how the world to evil allures me!
O how my heart is tempted to sin!
I must tell Jesus, and He will help me
Over the world the victory to win.
Refrain

The trials of others often inspire the creation of some of the most heartfelt songs and poems. Such was the case around the mid-1800s when the Reverend Elisha A. Hoffman of Pennsylvania visited home of a deeply distressed woman —distraught that her burdens had become too much for her to bear.

When he was not busy preparing a sermon or writing hymns, Hoffman frequently visited the poor and downcast in the homes of those he served.

"Coming to her home one day, I found her much discouraged," Hoffman later wrote .

After praying for the woman, Hoffman offered comfort through the scriptures, quoting "Come unto me all ye that labour and are heavy laden and I will give you rest." Still the woman was uneasy, asking the preacher over and over, "What shall I do? What shall I do?"

It was then that Hoffman offered the best advice possible: "Tell your sorrows to Jesus. You must tell Jesus."

For a moment she seemed lost in meditation. Then her eyes lit up as she exclaimed to Hoffman, "Yes, I must tell Jesus."

"As I left her home I had a vision of that joy-illuminated face. . . . and I heard all along my pathway the echo, 'I must tell Jesus. I must tell Jesus.'"[27]

Returning home, the conversation remained in Hoffman's thoughts. Realizing the truth of those words and acknowledging that it is not humanly possible for one to bear their burdens alone, Hoffman later sat down to write the words and music to this great song.

Today, as then, it is not humanly possible for one to bear the many burdens and trials that come. Jesus offers to take them. If we will let Him, He will lighten our loads..

I NEED THEE EVERY HOUR

ANNIE SHERWOOD HAWKS, 1872

I need Thee every hour, most gracious Lord;
No tender voice like Thine can peace afford.

> *I need Thee, O I need Thee;*
> *Every hour I need Thee;*
> *O bless me now, my Savior,*
> *I come to Thee.*

I need Thee every hour, stay Thou nearby;
Temptations lose their power when Thou art nigh.

> *I need Thee, O I need Thee;*
> *Every hour I need Thee;*
> *O bless me now, my Savior,*
> *I come to Thee.*

I need Thee every hour, in joy or pain;
Come quickly and abide, or life is in vain.

> *I need Thee, O I need Thee;*
> *Every hour I need Thee;*
> *O bless me now, my Savior,*
> *I come to Thee.*

I need Thee every hour; teach me Thy will;
And Thy rich promises in me fulfill.

> *I need Thee, O I need Thee;*
> *Every hour I need Thee;*
> *O bless me now, my Savior,*
> *I come to Thee.*

I need Thee every hour, most Holy One;
O make me Thine indeed, Thou blessèd Son.

I need Thee, O I need Thee;
Every hour I need Thee;
O bless me now, my Savior,
I come to Thee.

This song is taken from Psalm 86:7, "In the day of my trouble I will call upon thee: for thou wilt answer me." Annie Sherwood Hawks aptly described the yearning for God's help that led to the writing of this deeply personal hymn, which was written in 1872. A prolific writer from the age of fourteen, Hawks once recalled the thoughts that inspired the writing of this popular hymn.

"One day as a young wife and mother of thirty-seven years of age, I was busy with my regular household tasks during a bright June morning in 1872. Suddenly, I became so filled with the sense of nearness to the Master, and I began to wonder how anyone could live without Him, either in joy or pain. Then, the words were ushered into my mind and these thoughts took full possession of me—'I Need Thee Every Hour.'"[28]

Hawks wrote down the lyrics and later showed them to her pastor, well-known sacred music composer Robert Lowry, at the Hanson Place Baptist Church in New York. Robert Lowry wrote the music and in 1872 *I Need Thee Every Hour* was published at the National Baptist Sunday

School Convention in Cincinnati, Ohio. Years later, after the death of her husband, Hawks wrote:

"I did not understand at first why this hymn had touched the great throbbing heart of humanity. It was not until long years after, when the shadow fell over my way, the shadow of a great loss, that I understood something of the comforting power in the words which I had been permitted to give out to others in my hour of sweet serenity and peace."[29]

Hawks wrote more than 400 hymns before her death in 1918. Today, *I Need Thee Every Hour* rings loud and clear in churches across America, often as an invitational during altar calls. The heart of the message continues to speak to the hearts of people everywhere who recognize their need for a Savior.

HAVE THINE OWN WAY, LORD

ADELAIDE POLLARD

Have Thine own way, Lord! Have Thine own way!
Thou art the Potter, I am the clay.
Mold me and make me after Thy will,
While I am waiting, yielded and still.

Have Thine own way, Lord! Have Thine own way!
Search me and try me, Master, today!
Whiter than snow, Lord, wash me just now,
As in Thy presence humbly I bow.

Have Thine own way, Lord! Have Thine own way!
Wounded and weary, help me, I pray!
Power, all power, surely is Thine!
Touch me and heal me, Savior divine.

Have Thine own way, Lord! Have Thine own way!
Hold o'er my being absolute sway!
Fill with Thy Spirit 'till all shall see
Christ only, always, living in me.

As a missionary, Adelaide Pollard experienced a great burden for the country of Africa in 1907 and believed strongly that the Lord wanted her to minister there. Failing in her efforts to raise funds to finance the trip and confused as to why God had not stepped in to help, the 45-year-old Pollard was close to depression when she heard an elderly woman praying these simple words during a prayer meeting: "It doesn't matter what you bring into our lives, Lord;

just have Your own way with us."

Before that day in 1907, Pollard, like her mother before her, had written a number of spiritual hymns. Little did she know that the words she heard that night would inspire the creation of her most famous and one of the world's most loved hymns.

On her way home, perhaps still pondering her situation and questioning God, Pollard could not help but acknowledge the words that kept ringing in her head: "Have Thine own way." At home, she opened her Bible to the book of Jeremiah, where she read the account of a potter. "Then I went down to the potter's house, and, behold, he wrought a work on the wheels. And the vessel that he made of clay was marred in the hand of the potter: so he made it again another vessel, as seemed good to the potter to make it" (Jeremiah 18:3-4).

Perhaps my questions of God's will shows a flaw in my life, Pollard thought as she read over the scripture. So, God has decided to break me, as the potter broke the defective vessel, and then to mold my life again in His own pattern. Before retiring for bed, Pollard wrote a poem she titled "Have Thine Own Way." A short time later, the words were set to music and the hymn rang out to the Christian world.

In the years that followed, Pollard taught at the Christian and Missionary Alliance School in Nyack, New York. Shortly before World War I, she realized her dream and traveled to minister in Africa. Pollard wrote over 100 other songs before her death in 1934 at age 72.

Still a favorite in churches today, *Have Thine Own Way* serves as the ultimate response to God when answers to our questions seem so far away. Jesus recognized this as He prayed in the Garden at Gethsemane, saying: "Father, if thou be willing, remove this cup from me: nevertheless not my will, but thine, be done" (Luke 22:42).

MUST JESUS BEAR THE CROSS ALONE?

THOMAS SHEPHERD

Must Jesus bear the cross alone
And all the world go free?
No, there's a cross for everyone,
And there's a cross for me.

The consecrated cross I'll bear
Till death shall set me free,
And then go home my crown to wear,
For there's a crown for me.

Upon the crystal pavement, down
At Jesus' pierced feet,
Joyful I'll cast my golden crown
And His dear name repeat.

O precious cross! O glorious crown!
O resurrection day!
Ye angels, from the stars come down
And bear my soul away.

Though still a familiar hymn, often sung in churches during the altar call, not much is known about its origin. Written in 1693, the hymn reportedly got its title from a message preached by Thomas Shepherd, "Must Peter Bear the Cross Alone?" In the message, Shepherd preached about Simon Peter, who people believe was crucified upside down. It was a year later that Shepherd, deciding to take up the cause of the Cross, left his pastorate in the Church of England and became an independent preacher. Today the song still ushers us to receive Christ as our Savior and, like Shepherd, to take up the cross and follow Him.

HIS EYE IS ON THE SPARROW

CIVILLA D. MARTIN

Why should I feel discouraged? Why should the shadows come?
Why should my heart be lonely and long for Heav'n and home,
When Jesus is my portion? My constant Friend is He;
His eye is on the sparrow, and I know He watches me,
His eye is on the sparrow, and I know He watches me.

I sing because I'm happy,
I sing because I'm free,
For His eye is on the sparrow,
And I know He watches me.

"Let not your heart be troubled," His tender word I hear,
And resting on His goodness, I lose my doubts and fears;
Tho' by the path He leadeth but one step I may see;
His eye is on the sparrow, and I know He watches me;
His eye is on the sparrow, and I know He watches me.

I sing because I'm happy,
I sing because I'm free,
For His eye is on the sparrow,
And I know He watches me.

Whenever I am tempted, whenever clouds arise,
When songs give place to sighing, when hope within me dies,
I draw the closer to Him, from care He sets me free;
His eye is on the sparrow, and I know He cares for me;
His eye is on the sparrow, and I know He cares for me.

I sing because I'm happy,
I sing because I'm free,
For His eye is on the sparrow,
And I know He watches me.

"Are not two sparrows sold for a farthing? and one of them shall not fall on the ground without your Father. But the very hairs of your head are all numbered. Fear ye not therefore, ye are of more value than many sparrows" (Matthew 10:29-31). This familiar passage of scripture may have been the true inspiration behind this popular church song. But it was the faith of a seriously ill woman that led Civilla D. Martin to pen the hymn in the early 1900s.

In the spring of 1905, Mrs. Martin and her husband visited a couple in Elmira, New York. The wife had been bedridden for nearly 20 years and the husband was restricted to a wheelchair. Despite their afflictions, the couple was happy and inspired others with their faith and determination.

Recalling what prompted her to write the song, Martin once said, "One day while we were visiting with the Doolittles, my husband commented on their bright hopefulness and asked them for the secret of it. Mrs. Doolittle's reply was simple: 'His eye is on the sparrow, and I know He watches me.'

"The beauty of this simple expression of boundless faith gripped the hearts and fired the imagination of Dr. Martin and me," Mrs. Martin said.[30]

The hymn *His Eye Is on the Sparrow* was the result of that experience and the following day Martin wrote the words in the form of a poem. She mailed the poem to a friend, Charles Gabriel, who put the words to music.

In the years since, this song has become a comfort to many who, like the Doolittles, experience similar trouble and sickness. Similarly, we should not be discouraged. Not as long as we know that Jesus is still our portion and constant Friend. Just as His eye is on the sparrow, He is also watching over us.

What a Friend We Have in Jesus

Joseph M. Scriven, 1855

What a Friend we have in Jesus, all our sins and griefs to bear!
What a privilege to carry everything to God in prayer!
O what peace we often forfeit, O what needless pain we bear,
All because we do not carry everything to God in prayer.

Have we trials and temptations? Is there trouble anywhere?
We should never be discouraged; take it to the Lord in prayer.
Can we find a friend so faithful who will all our sorrows share?
Jesus knows our every weakness; take it to the Lord in prayer.

Are we weak and heavy laden, cumbered with a load of care?
Precious Savior, still our refuge, take it to the Lord in prayer.
Do your friends despise, forsake you? Take it to the Lord in prayer!
In His arms He'll take and shield you; you will find a solace there.

Blessed Savior, Thou hast promised Thou wilt all our burdens bear.
May we ever, Lord, be bringing all to Thee in earnest prayer.
Soon in glory bright unclouded there will be no need for prayer.
Rapture, praise and endless worship will be our sweet portion there.

Some of the best-known spirituals and hymns were borne out of sorrow and tragedy. Such was the case with this popular tune, which Joseph M. Scriven wrote in 1855 as a poem to his mother, who was sick. Although apparently meant to comfort her, the lyrics suggest that Scriven, who had suffered the tragic loss of two fiancés, might have been encouraging himself as well.

Born in Dublin, Ireland, in 1819, Scriven met and fell in love with a young woman. On the evening of their wedding she accidentally drowned. Some years later, Scriven settled in Canada where he performed menial tasks for poor widows and the sick. While there, he met another woman and again planned to be married. Tragedy struck a second time—the woman contracted pneumonia and died.

In 1855, Scriven had himself become ill. A friend visited Scriven and found the poem Scriven had written to his mother. He had titled the poem, "Pray Without Ceasing." He asked Scriven about the poem, and the ailing man answered, "The Lord and I did it between us."[31]

In 1868, musician Charles Converse put the words of Scriven's poem to music and titled it *What a Friend We Have in Jesus.* When Scriven died some 18 years later in an accidental drowning, the town of Port Hope erected a monument that was inscribed with a portion of his now famous song: "In His arms He'll take and shield thee. Thou wilt find a solace there."

Those words are still bringing comfort to many today as God, our shield, continues to give us peace.

LEANING ON THE EVERLASTING ARMS

ANTHONY J. SHOWALTER, WITH ELISHA A. HOFFMAN

What a fellowship, what a joy divine,
Leaning on the everlasting arms;
What a blessedness, what a peace is mine,
Leaning on the everlasting arms.

Leaning, leaning, safe and secure from all alarms;
Leaning, leaning, leaning on the everlasting arms.

Oh, how sweet to walk in this pilgrim way,
Leaning on the everlasting arms;
Oh, how bright the path grows from day to day,
Leaning on the everlasting arms.

Leaning, leaning, safe and secure from all alarms;
Leaning, leaning, leaning on the everlasting arms.

What have I to dread, what have I to fear,
Leaning on the everlasting arms?
I have blessed peace with my Lord so near,
Leaning on the everlasting arms.

Leaning, leaning, safe and secure from all alarms;
Leaning, leaning, leaning on the everlasting arms.

Another great song borne out of tragedy, the tune and words of this popular song were written in 1887 after Anthony J. Showalter received word that the wives of two of his friends had died. Before writing the song, Showalter reflected on a verse of scripture from Deuteronomy 33:27: "The eternal God is thy refuge, and underneath are the everlasting arms: and he shall thrust out the enemy from before thee; and shall say, Destroy them."

For help with the remaining lyrics, Showalter called on Elisha A. Hoffman, the author of more than 2,000 gospel hymns. Like many of his lyrics, these offer comfort to those seeking closeness to God and a peace that only He can give. Their comfort is in knowing that He is near and that He gives you peace. And what could be more indicative of peace than the knowledge that we can lean on God's everlasting arms?

PASS ME NOT, O GENTLE SAVIOR

FANNY CROSBY

Pass me not, O gentle Savior,
Hear my humble cry;
While on others Thou art calling,
Do not pass me by.

Savior, Savior,
Hear my humble cry;
While on others Thou art calling,
Do not pass me by.

Let me at Thy throne of mercy
Find a sweet relief,
Kneeling there in deep contrition;
Help my unbelief.

Savior, Savior,
Hear my humble cry;
While on others Thou art calling,
Do not pass me by.

Trusting only in Thy merit,
Would I seek Thy face;
Heal my wounded, broken spirit,
Save me by Thy grace.

Savior, Savior,
Hear my humble cry;
While on others Thou art calling,
Do not pass me by.

Thou the Spring of all my comfort,
More than life to me,
Whom have I on earth beside Thee?
Whom in heav'n but Thee?

Savior, Savior,
Hear my humble cry;
While on others Thou art calling,
Do not pass me by.

Of the more than 8,000 hymns written by Fanny Crosby, *Pass Me Not, O Gentle Savior* became her most popular, written in 1886. The story goes that Crosby, who wrote as many as three hymns a week for use in a Sunday school publication, based this hymn on a prayer she heard someone pray at a church service. Her hymns were aimed at bringing the message of the Gospel to people who would not listen to preaching. Whenever she wrote a hymn, she prayed that God would use it to lead many souls to Him.

One incident that supports this is the story of a wayward young man and how he changed his ways after hearing Crosby's hymn. A concerned Christian pastor approached the young man, seeking to influence him to seek God. Meeting him one day, the loving pastor sought once more to influence him, urging, "We want you for Christ and His service." There was a certain change in his manner which did not escape the eye of the prayerful watcher for souls, and—lacking time to do more—he seized the opportunity to secure the presence of his young friend at a Christian Endeavor meeting.

True to his promise the young man was there. When an opportunity was given for some of the young men to choose a song, it was seen that he was urging his companion to select a particular hymn. The other, yielding to his request, asked if the hymn, *Pass Me Not, O Gentle Saviour*, might be sung; and both young men joined in the singing with evident interest and heartiness. Later in the evening it was requested that all who were definitely on the Lord's side would confess their allegiance by standing, whereupon the one for whom the heart of the pastor was specially yearning rose at once, and with decision.

"Tell me about your conversion," the thankful pastor requested at the close of the meeting, when hands were clasped in glad, brotherly welcome and recognition.

"Oh, yes," assented the other. "It was all through that hymn we have just sung. I was working on the canal . . . and there was a meeting being held at the Mariner's Chapel nearby. The words floated out over the water, and from the tug where I was working I could hear them plainly enough. When they were just going to sing those lines—'While on others Thou art calling, Do not pass me by!' a great fear came over me, and I thought, 'Oh, if the Lord were to pass me by, how terrible it would be!' Then and there, on the tug, I cried out, 'O Lord, do not pass me by.' And"—he said with a bright smile—"He didn't pass me by. I am saved."[32]

I Surrender All

JUDSON W. VAN DE VENTER

All to Jesus I surrender,
All to Him I freely give;
I will ever love and trust Him,
In His presence daily live.

I surrender all,
I surrender all.
All to Thee, my blessed Savior,
I surrender all.

All to Jesus I surrender,
Humbly at His feet I bow,
Worldly pleasures all forsaken,
Take me, Jesus, take me now.

I surrender all,
I surrender all.
All to Thee, my blessed Savior,
I surrender all.

All to Jesus I surrender,
Make me, Savior, wholly Thine;
Let me feel the Holy Spirit,
Truly know that Thou art mine.

I surrender all,
I surrender all.
All to Thee, my blessed Savior,
I surrender all.
All to Jesus I surrender,
Lord, I give myself to Thee;

Fill me with Thy love and power,
Let Thy blessing fall on me.

I surrender all,
I surrender all.
All to Thee, my blessed Savior,
I surrender all.

For five years, Judson W. Van De Venter wandered in confusion, undecided as to whether he should continue his work as a successful art teacher or give it all up to pursue full-time evangelism. Although a number of church friends who had noticed Van De Venter's gifts in counseling and working with people had urged him along the lines of evangelism, his direction had to come from the Lord. And it did.

"At last the pivotal hour of my life came and I surrendered all," Van De Venter wrote. "A new day was ushered into my life. I became an evangelist and discovered down deep in my soul a talent hitherto unknown to me. God had hidden a song in my heart, and touching a chord He caused me to sing songs I had never sung before."

A short time after this experience, Van De Venter wrote *I Surrender All*, a song of surrender that expressed his willingness to submit to whatever the Lord had in store for his life. Winfield Scott Weeden, a publisher, wrote the music for the song. His reaction to the song was so great he had its title engraved on his tombstone.

Frequently sung today as song of surrender during

altar calls, *I Surrender All* still serves as a strong invitation to those seeking God with a willing heart—those who are willing to give up everything to become His disciples.

IT IS WELL WITH MY SOUL

HORATIO SPAFFORD

When peace, like a river, attendeth my way,
When sorrows like sea billows roll;
Whatever my lot, Thou has taught me to say,
It is well, it is well, with my soul.
It is well, with my soul,
It is well, with my soul,
It is well, it is well, with my soul.
Though Satan should buffet, though trials should come,
Let this blest assurance control,
That Christ has regarded my helpless estate,
And hath shed His own blood for my soul.
It is well, with my soul,
It is well, with my soul,
It is well, it is well, with my soul.
My sin, oh, the bliss of this glorious thought!
My sin, not in part but the whole,
Is nailed to the cross, and I bear it no more,
Praise the Lord, praise the Lord, O my soul!
It is well, with my soul,
It is well, with my soul,
It is well, it is well, with my soul.
For me, be it Christ, be it Christ hence to live:
If Jordan above me shall roll,
No pang shall be mine, for in death as in life
Thou wilt whisper Thy peace to my soul.
It is well, with my soul,
It is well, with my soul,
It is well, it is well, with my soul.
But, Lord, 'tis for Thee, for Thy coming we wait,
The sky, not the grave, is our goal;
Oh trump of the angel! Oh voice of the Lord!

> *Blessèd hope, blessèd rest of my soul!*
> *It is well, with my soul,*
> *It is well, with my soul,*
> *It is well, it is well, with my soul.*
> *And Lord, haste the day when my faith shall be sight,*
> *The clouds be rolled back as a scroll;*
> *The trump shall resound, and the Lord shall descend,*
> *Even so, it is well with my soul.*
> *It is well, with my soul,*
> *It is well, with my soul,*
> *It is well, it is well, with my soul.*

"Saved alone."

These words, sent to businessman Horatio Spafford in a telegram in November 1873, might have been interpreted as good news and they were. Spafford's wife, Anna, had survived a devastating collision of two ships that took place as the vessels crossed the Atlantic Ocean.

But the message represented more than just a report of one life that was saved. The telegram delivered the sad news that Spafford's four daughters, who were traveling with their mother, had all been killed in the collision. Two hundred and twenty-two others also died when the ships collided.

This accident was the last in a string of tragic events that affected Spafford's otherwise successful life during the 1870s. A successful Chicago lawyer and a close friend of evangelist Dwight L. Moody, Spafford watched all of his holdings go up in flames following the devastating Chicago fire of 1871. Prior to that, Spafford's son had died.

Spafford, his wife, and daughters had decided to get away for a while and vacation in England where they would visit with Moody. Business matters prevented Spafford from leaving immdediately, so he sent his family ahead with plans of joining them in a few days.

Several weeks passed before Spafford was able to board a ship to join his grieving wife in Cardiff, Wales. As his ship passed near the spot where his daughters had died, Spafford stood on deck gazing over the mighty waters that had claimed their lives. When he returned to his cabin, Spafford wrote the following words:

When peace, like a river, attendeth my way,
When sorrows like sea billows roll,
Whatever my lot, Thou hast taught me to say,
It is well, it is well, with my soul.

Though written in the midst of sorrow, the words brought solace to Spafford at a time when he did not know where else to find peace. The words that followed brought additional comfort.

Though Satan should buffet, though trials should come,
Let this blessed assurance control,
That Christ hath regarded my helpless estate,
And hath shed His own blood for my soul.

The words of this timeless song still speak eternal hope to all believers, no matter what the pain, hurt, or loss. We still have God's assurance that He is with us and there is no reason to fear. We can still say, "It is well with my soul."

I HEARD THE VOICE OF JESUS SAY

DR. HORATIUS BONAR

I heard the voice of Jesus say, "Come unto Me and rest;
Lay down, thou weary one, lay down, Thy head upon My breast."

I came to Jesus as I was, weary and worn and sad;
I found in Him a resting place, and He has made me glad.

I heard the voice of Jesus say, "Behold, I freely give
The living water; thirsty one, stoop down, and drink, and live."

I came to Jesus, and I drank of that life-giving stream;
My thirst was quenched, my soul revived, and now I live in Him.

I heard the voice of Jesus say, "I am this dark world's Light;
Look unto Me, thy morn shall rise, and all thy day be bright."

I looked to Jesus, and I found in Him my Star, my Sun;
And in that light of life I'll walk, till traveling days are done.

The famous hymn writer Dr. Horatius Bonar was forever doodling on envelopes and in notepads he carried in
his pockets, jotting down lines of hymns whenever they
came to him. His notepads were filled as much with carica-
tures and other sketches as they were with lines of poetry
that Bonar eventually turned into songs.

Though Bonar loved hymns, he met with much opposition from adult church members who favored the singing of
psalms. Some were resistant to the point of walking out of
the service when hymns were sung. Consequently, Bonar

spent considerable time singing with the children in the Sunday school before delivering his sermons on Sunday mornings.

Bonar found peace, comfort, and a place for his music among the children that he could not realize with the adult congregation. It was that peace, perhaps, that led him to write this hymn during the 1840s expressly for the children of his Sunday school class.

While the words of numerous songs popularized by such composers as Bonar were changed throughout the years, not a word of this well-known hymn has been altered or adjusted since Bonar scribbled the twelve lines in one of his notebooks and doodled on the margins four incomplete faces and the head of a man wearing a hat.

Like the simple hymn written long ago, the message has not changed. Jesus is still offering to comfort us as we go to Him for rest from the weariness of everyday trials and pressures.

NEAR THE CROSS

FANNY CROSBY

Jesus, keep me near the cross;
There a precious fountain,
Free to all—a healing stream—
Flows from Calvary's mountain.

In the cross, in the cross,
Be my glory ever;
Till my raptured soul shall find
Rest beyond the river.

Near the cross, a trembling soul,
Love and mercy found me;
There the bright and morning star
Shed its beams around me.

In the cross, in the cross,
Be my glory ever;
Till my raptured soul shall find
Rest beyond the river.

Near the cross! O Lamb of God,
Bring its scenes before me;
Help me walk from day to day
With its shadow o'er me.

In the cross, in the cross,
Be my glory ever;
Till my raptured soul shall find
Rest beyond the river.

Near the cross I'll watch and wait,

Hoping, trusting ever,
Till I reach the golden strand
Just beyond the river.

In the cross, in the cross,
Be my glory ever;
Till my raptured soul shall find
Rest beyond the river.

Little is known about this inspirational hymn that was written early in the career of Frances Jane (Fanny) Crosby, other than that Crosby wrote it at the request of a friend, William Howard Doane, who wanted words added to a tune he had written.

The woman many called "Aunt Fanny" is recognized as perhaps the most prolific hymnist in history. Though blind from the time she was six weeks old, Crosby wrote thousands of hymns, taught school, and befriended some of the highest-ranking dignitaries in the country, including generals and presidents. Her greatest hymns include *Safe in the Arms of Jesus* and *Blessed Assurance*.

It is likely that her blindness helped Crosby to stay focused on her Savior and "near the cross." Of her blindness, Crosby once said: "It seemed intended by the blessed providence of God that I should be blind all my life, and I thank Him for the dispensation. If perfect earthly sight were offered me tomorrow, I would not accept it. I might not have sung hymns to the praise of God if I had been distracted by the beautiful and interesting things about me."[33]

As it was for Crosby, *Near the Cross* is a reminder for us to get back to the basics of Christianity. One of the strengths of the African-American church is its foundation on the simplicity of the gospel message. Songs such as this were instrumental in reminding them of the roots of their faith.

Crosby died in her sleep at age 94. Many of the hymns she wrote are still included in church hymnals today. They stand as a testament to the rich legacy she left behind—a reminder to the world that even in darkness we can still draw near to God. It is there that we find peace and safety.

MASTER, THE TEMPEST IS RAGING!

MARY A. BAKER, 1874

Master, the tempest is raging!
The billows are tossing high!
The sky is o'ershadowed with blackness,
No shelter or help is nigh;
Carest Thou not that we perish?
How canst Thou lie asleep,
When each moment so madly is threatening
A grave in the angry deep?
The winds and the waves obey Thy will,
Peace, be still!

Whether the wrath of the storm-tossed sea,
Or demons or men, or whatever it be,
No waters can swallow the ship where lies
The Master of ocean, and earth, and skies;
They all shall sweetly obey Thy will,
Peace, be still! Peace, be still!
They all shall sweetly obey Thy will,
Peace, peace, be still!

Master, with anguish of spirit
I bow in my grief today;
The depths of my sad heart are troubled,
Oh, waken and save, I pray!
Torrents of sin and of anguish
Sweep o'er my sinking soul;
And I perish! I perish! dear Master,
Oh, hasten, and take control.
The winds and the waves obey Thy will,
Peace, be still!

Whether the wrath of the storm-tossed sea,
Or demons or men, or whatever it be,
No waters can swallow the ship where lies
The Master of ocean, and earth, and skies;
They all shall sweetly obey Thy will,
Peace, be still! Peace, be still!
They all shall sweetly obey Thy will,
Peace, peace, be still!

Master, the terror is over,
The elements sweetly rest;
Earth's sun in the calm lake is mirrored,
And heaven's within my breast;
Linger, O blessèd Redeemer!
Leave me alone no more;
And with joy I shall make the blest harbor,
And rest on the blissful shore.
The winds and the waves obey Thy will,
Peace, be still!
Whether the wrath of the storm-tossed sea,
Or demons or men, or whatever it be,
No waters can swallow the ship where lies
The Master of ocean, and earth, and skies;
They all shall sweetly obey Thy will,
Peace, be still! Peace, be still!
They all shall sweetly obey Thy will,
Peace, peace, be still!

A Sunday school lesson recounting the Bible story of
Christ calming the sea and the remembrance of her brother's death served as the inspiration for this powerful hymn,
written in 1874 by Mary A. Baker. Baker, a Baptist, prepared several songs to accompany a lesson titled "Christ

Stilling the Tempest" that she presented to her Sunday school class.

"It so expressed an experience I had recently passed through that this hymn was the result. A very dear and only brother, a young man of rare loveliness and promise of character, had been laid in the grave, a victim of the same disease that had already taken father and mother," Baker wrote.

"His death occurred under peculiarly distressing circumstances. He was more than a thousand miles away from home, seeking in the balmy air of the sunny South the healing that our colder climate could not give. Suddenly he grew worse . . . ."

Unable to go and see about him, Baker and her sisters spent two weeks exchanging telegrams with their brother—keeping up with his condition.

"Ere the word came which told us that our beloved brother was no longer a dweller on the earth," Baker wrote. "Although we mourned not as those without hope, and although I had believed on Christ in early childhood and had always desired to give the Master a consecrated and obedient life, I became wickedly rebellious at this dispensation of divine providence. I said in my heart that God did not care for me or mine."[34]

The rebellion didn't last long, however. Baker found quick forgiveness in the arms of a loving Master whose "own voice stilled the tempest in my unsanctified heart, and brought it to the calm of a deeper faith and a more perfect trust." As Jesus had so forcefully spoken peace to a troubling storm, He was now speaking the same to Baker's heart, saying, "Peace, be still." In the quiet moments that followed, Baker wrote of that peace in a song that still brings comfort today.

MARCHING TO ZION

ISAAC WATTS

Come, we that love the Lord,
And let our joys be known;
Join in a song with sweet accord,
Join in a song with sweet accord,
And thus surround the throne,
And thus surround the throne.

We're marching to Zion,
Beautiful, beautiful Zion;
We're marching upward to Zion,
The beautiful city of God.
The sorrows of the mind
Be banished from the place;
Religion never was designed,
Religion never was designed,
To make our pleasures less,
To make our pleasures less.

Let those refuse to sing,
Who never knew our God;
But favorites of the heavenly King,
But favorites of the heavenly King
May speak their joys abroad,
May speak their joys abroad.
(chorus)

The God that rules on high,
And thunders when He please,
Who rides upon the stormy sky,
Who rides upon the stormy sky,
And manages the seas,

And manages the seas.
(chorus)

This awful God is ours,
Our Father and our Love;
He will send down his heav'nly powers,
He will send down his heav'nly powers,
To carry us above,
To carry us above.
(chorus)

There we shall see His face,
And never, never sin!
There, from the rivers of His grace,
There, from the rivers of His grace,
Drink endless pleasures in,
Drink endless pleasures in.
(chorus)

Yea, and before we rise,
To that immortal state,
The thoughts of such amazing bliss,
The thoughts of such amazing bliss,
Should constant joys create,
Should constant joys create.
(chorus)

The men of grace have found,
Glory begun below.
Celestial fruits on earthly ground
Celestial fruits on earthly ground
From faith and hope may grow,
From faith and hope may grow.
(chorus)

The hill of Zion yields
A thousand sacred sweets
Before we reach the heav'nly fields,
Before we reach the heav'nly fields,
Or walk the golden streets,
Or walk the golden streets.
(chorus)

Then let our songs abound,
And every tear be dry;
We're marching through Immanuel's ground,
We're marching through Immanuel's ground,
To fairer worlds on high,
To fairer worlds on high.
(chorus)

One need only look to the third stanza of this controversial yet worshipful hymn to realize that Isaac Watts desired to convey a message when he wrote it in the mid-1800s.

Reportedly, a controversy arose among many of the congregants over whether to sing psalms or hymns. The church decided to sing psalms at the beginning of the service and follow the preaching with hymns. Those who opposed the singing of hymns in the church would get up and leave the service at the point the hymns would begin. As a way of combating this practice, Watts expressed in this hymn the position that those who "truly" love the Lord would not hesitate to sing hymns of praise to Him.

In his own way, Watts invites true worshippers to "let our joys be known," while establishing that religion was not designed to be burdensome, but rather a joy. When we gather in the house of worship, we give praise to God in a variety of ways. That is the time to "sing psalms and hymns and spiritual songs among yourselves, making music to the Lord in your hearts" (Ephesians 5:19 NLT).

THE VOICES BEHIND THE MUSIC:

BIOGRAPHIES OF H.T. BURLEIGH, HARRIET TUBMAN, CHARLES TINDLEY, JAMES WELDON JOHNSON, AND THOMAS A. DORSEY

H. T. BURLEIGH

Henry Thacker Burleigh was born in Erie, Pennsylvania on December 2, 1866. Because his mother, Elizabeth, was unable to find a teaching position despite her college education and fluency in French and Greek, she made her living as a domestic worker. Burleigh's interest in music can be traced back to his maternal grandfather. As he performed his duties as the town crier and lamplighter, Hamilton Waters sang plantation songs to young Henry, thus passing on a music which would one day become known as the spiritual. Henry's mother, who Burleigh later recognized as his strongest supporter, was also aware of his passion for music. Elizabeth gained permission from her employer for Henry to act as doorkeeper when guests arrived so that he could listen to the musical entertainment.

During his youth and young adulthood, Burleigh took several jobs to support his family. However, music was his constant companion. In 1892, Burleigh auditioned for a scholarship to the National Conservatory of Music in New York. Due to the intervention of the registrar, Frances MacDowell, Burleigh received the scholarship. Burleigh made many influential contacts during his years at the conservatory but none were more important than his association with the Czech composer, Antonin Dvo_ák, who became director of the conservatory in 1892. Burleigh spent many evenings singing the spirituals of his youth for Dvo_ák and also did manuscript copying for the composer.

In 1894, Burleigh auditioned for the baritone soloist position at

St. George's Episcopal Church of New York. Although there was much debate about hiring a Negro to sing in such an affluent parish, he was selected for the post. The beginning of this 52-year relationship marked the first time that Burleigh's income enabled him to concentrate on his music. Burleigh completed his studies at the conservatory in 1896 and went on to become one of the best-known African-American composers of all time. The estimates of the number of songs Burleigh wrote range from two to three hundred. Burleigh died of heart failure on September 12, 1949. His funeral, held at St. George's, was attended by two thousand mourners.

HARRIET TUBMAN

Harriet Ross was born into slavery around 1820 in Maryland. She was raised under a harsh master and given frequent whippings even as a small child. At the age of 25, she married John Tubman, a free African American. Five years later, because she feared being sold and sent further into the South, Harriet decided to escape to Canada. With the assistance of those involved in the Underground Railroad, Harriet reached the safety of Pennsylvania. Once there, she made the acquaintance of William Still, Philadelphia stationmaster on the Underground Railroad (UGRR). In 1851, she became the conductor in St. Catherines, Ontario and began bringing members of her family out of slavery. In all, she is believed to have conducted approximately three hundred persons to freedom in the North. The tales of her exploits reveal her dependence on God, as well as her grim determination to protect her charges and those who helped them. Tubman was a close associate of many well-known abolitionists, including John Brown, Frederick Douglass, Jermain Loguen, and Gerrit Smith. During the Civil War, Tubman served as a soldier, spy, and nurse. After the war ended, Tubman returned to Auburn, New York and married Nelson Davis. Once established in Auburn, Tubman became an advocate for women's rights and in 1908 built the structure that became her home for the aged and indigent. There she worked and was cared for herself in the years before her death in 1913.

CHARLES TINDLEY

Charles A. Tindley was born in Berlin, Maryland on July 7, 1851. He was born on a farm where his father was a slave and his mother was free born. Though his mother died when he was young, Tindley was raised by a sister until he was old enough to hire out as a laborer. Tindley had no formal education and taught himself to read and write. He worked as a janitor to put himself through night school, while earning a divinity degree by correspondence.

In 1902, he became pastor of a small 130-member church. The congregation grew to around 10,000 members and included both blacks and whites. In addition to being an exceptional preacher, Tindley was called "the people's pastor" and known for his pioneering song writing abilities. His soulful lyrics advocated love, patience, and tolerance. One of his best-known hymns, "I Shall Overcome," was modified to become the anthem for the Civil Rights Movement. Although Tindley was technically a musical illiterate, he wrote more than thirty hymns and is often referred to as the "father of gospel music."

JAMES WELDON JOHNSON

Songwriter, poet, novelist, journalist, critic, and auto-biographer James Weldon Johnson was born in Jacksonville, Florida in 1871. Johnson graduated from high school at the age of sixteen, attended college at Atlanta University, and then returned to his high school in 1894 to become its principal. Johnson then experimented with journalism when he started his own paper, the Daily American, in 1895 to report on important issues within the black community. The paper lasted just one year, after which Johnson decided to pursue a career in law. While retaining his position as principal, he built a successful practice. However, after Johnson's brother Rosamond returned from the New England Conservatory of Music in 1897 they began collaborating to write songs. Their best-known song, Lift Every Voice and Sing, was written for a school celebration while James was still in Florida. By 1900 the brothers were both in New York providing compositions to Broadway musicals. Johnson became well-known in the political realm, both as the American consul to Venezuela and the field secretary of the NAACP. He also played an important part of the Harlem Renaissance and became a prominent voice in the literary arena with his roles as writer, poet, and critic. Though he died in a tragic accident in 1938, Johnson continues to be remembered for personal integrity and devotion to human service.

THOMAS A. DORSEY

Born in 1899 in Villa Rica, Georgia, Thomas Dorsey's father was a Baptist pastor and his mother the church organist. In 1908, the family moved to Atlanta where they experienced some tough financial hardships. Dorsey felt isolated from his peers and sought refuge in the black community of downtown Atlanta. He left school at age eleven and found a job at the local vaudeville theater, where he taught himself to read music and play piano. In 1916, Dorsey joined the Great Migration North and moved to

Chicago where he found success almost immediately by playing the blues. Dorsey led a very hectic life in the nightlife of Chicago and by 1925 had suffered two nervous breakdowns. He was forced to spend a few years back in Georgia recovering in his parent's house. At the urging of his mother and his health, Dorsey began to compose sacred music in 1928. However, the widespread rejection of his music by mainstream churches forced him to his career in playing blues. In 1932, Dorsey's life was thrown into crisis when his wife and son died during childbirth. He turned to his piano for comfort and, inspired by God, composed the now-famous Take My Hand, Precious Lord. After co-founding the National Convention of Gospel Choirs and Choruses in 1933, Dorsey teamed up with Mahalia Jackson and together they ushered in the "Golden Age of Gospel Music." Dorsey himself came to be known as the "father of gospel music" and died in 1993.

INDEX

ENDNOTES

1. Dr. Wyatt T. Walker, *Somebody's Calling My Name,* Philadelphia: Judson Press, 1983.

2. Ibid.

3. Ibid.

4. Solomon Northup, *Twelve Years a Slave: Narrative of Solomon Northup, a Citizen of New York, Kidnapped in Washington City in 1841 and Rescued in 1853,* Auburn: Derby and Miller, 1853, p. 213.

5. *Texas Narratives: Ex-slave stories,* vol. 16, part 1 of *Born in Slavery: Slave Narratives from the Federal Writers' Project,* Library of Congress, 1936-1938, p. 199.

6. www.volcano.net/~jackmearl/hymns/phymns/precious_lord_take_my.htm

7. Bernice Johnson Reagon, *We'll Understand It Better By and By: Pioneering African-American Gospel Composers,* Washington and London: Smithsonian Institute Press, 1992, p. 336.

8. Ibid.

9. Ibid., p. 45.

10. Ibid., p. 115.

11. Ibid., p. 333.

12. Ibid., p. 46.

13. Ibid.

14. Ibid.

15. Bernice Johnson Reagon, "Lucie E. Campbell Williams: A Cultural Biography by Rev. Charles Walker," *We'll Understand It Better By and By: Pioneering African-American Gospel Composers*, Washington and London: Smithsonian Institute Press, 1992, p. 129.

16. Ibid.

17. Ibid.

18. Ibid., p. 131.

19. Ibid., p. 21.

20. http://www.appleseedrec.com/petecd/bruce.html

21. http://www.naacp.org/work/library/jamesweldon-johnson.shtml

22. Ibid.

23. *The Enchiridion*, "Isaac Watts: Hymns & Spiritual Songs, 1707-1709," London: Printed by J. Humfreys, for John Lawrence at the Angel in the Poultrey, 1707.

24. Kenneth W. Osbeck, *Singing With Understanding: Including 101 Favorite Hymn Backgrounds,* Grand Rapids: Kregel Publications, 1979, p. 62.

25. Ibid., p. 89.

26. Ibid.

27. Clint Bonner, *A Hymn Is Born*, Nashville: Broadman Press, 1959, p. 145.

28. http://www.cyberhymnal.org/htm/i/n/ineedteh.htm

29. Ibid.

30. http://geocities.com/t_tull/sparrow.htm

31. Kenneth W. Osbeck, *Singing With Understanding: Including 101 Favorite Hymn Backgrounds*, Grand Rapids: Kregel Publications, 1979,
p. 310.

32. http://www.cyberhymnal.org/htm/p/a/passment.htm

33. http://www.cyberhymnal.org/bio/c/r/crosby_fj.htm

34. http://www.cyberhymnal.org/htm/m/a/mastertt.htm

Additional copies of this book and other titles from Honor Books
are available from your local bookstore.

Also available in the African American Series:

Soul Cry:
Powerful Prayers from the Spiritual Heritage of African Americans

God Has Soul:
Celebrating the Indomitable Spirit of African Americans

Voices of Hope:
Timeless Expressions of Faith from African Americans

If you have enjoyed this book, or if it has impacted your life,
we would like to hear from you.

Please contact us at:

Honor Books

An imprint of Cook Communications Ministries

4050 Lee Vance View

Colorado Springs, CO 80918

www.cookministries.com